FLOURISHING

FLOURISHING

A Frank Conversation About Sustainability

John R. Ehrenfeld and Andrew J. Hoffman

STANFORD BUSINESS BOOKS
An Imprint of Stanford University Press
Stanford, California

Stanford University Press
Stanford, California

Special discounts for bulk quantities of Stanford Business Books are available to corporations, professional associations, and other organizations. For details and discount information, contact the special sales department of Stanford University Press. Tel: (650) 736-1782, Fax: (650) 736-1784

All chapter-opening images courtesy of Morphart Creations inc./Shutterstock.com.

Printed in the United States of America on acid-free, archival-quality paper

Library of Congress Cataloging-in-Publication Data

Ehrenfeld, John, interviewee.
  Flourishing : a frank conversation about sustainability / John R. Ehrenfeld and Andrew J. Hoffman.
      pages cm
  Includes bibliographical references and index.
  ISBN 978-0-8047-8414-6 (cloth : alk. paper) — ISBN 978-0-8047-8415-3 (pbk. : alk. paper)
  1. Sustainability. 2. Sustainable development. 3. Ehrenfeld, John—Interviews. I. Hoffman, Andrew J., 1961- interviewer. II. Title.
  HC79.E5.E36465 2013
  338.9'27—dc23

                        2013000654

ISBN 978-0-8047-8667-6 (electronic)

Published simultaneously in the UK by
Greenleaf Publishing Limited
Aizlewood's Mill
Nursery Street
Sheffield S3 8GG
www.greenleaf-publishing.com

A catalogue record for this book is available from the British Library.
ISBN-13: 978-1-906093-93-8 (paperback)

Typeset by Bruce Lundquist in 10.5/15 Adobe Garamond

Contents

Preface   vii

1. Introduction   1

I. CLARIFYING THE ISSUE

2. Sustainability Means Nothing Without an End in Sight   15

3. The Myths of Our Modern Culture   29

4. The Wrong-Headed Solutions of Corporate Sustainability   49

5. More Is Not Better   67

II. LIVING WITH A DIFFERENT STORY

6. Reexamining What It Means to Be Human   81

7. Returning to Our Place in the Whole   99

III. LOOKING TO THE FUTURE

8. Reasons to Be Hopeful   119

Recommended Readings and Bibliography   138

About the Authors   143

Index   145

Preface

"Teaching is more difficult than learning because what teaching calls for is this: to let learn. The real teacher, in fact, lets nothing else be learned than learning. His conduct, therefore, often produces the impression that we properly learn nothing from him, if by 'learning' we now suddenly understand merely the procurement of useful information."

—*Martin Heidegger*

What is the legacy of a professor? This is a question that every professor asks him- or herself at some point in their career. How do we know if we have left an imprint on our students? How do we know if our ideas and research will make a difference in the world? The answers to these questions are elusive, and often require an element of faith; trust that our ideas will live beyond us and grow within those whom we touch through our teaching and writing. But in Martin Heidegger's words we can see a glimpse of where a more precise answer can be found. A great professor teaches his students to learn and continue to learn.

On that measure, John Ehrenfeld has left a large legacy. John saw the importance of environmental issues to business long before others did, and he devoted his life to researching and teaching them. But, more important, he nurtured others to carry on his work. It is not an idle boast to say that John is responsible for populating today's business schools with more professors focused on the environment and sustainability than produced by any other teacher. Today, John's students teach at the London Business School, University of Virginia, Dartmouth College,

University of Rochester, University of Oregon, Melbourne Business School, and University of Michigan. In fact, when I ask John what he sees as the measure of his legacy, he is quick to answer, "My legacy is my students." In full disclosure, I am one of those students, and this book is a testament to his work; a walk through John's ideas from his perspective and through my eyes and ears.

I first met John in 1991 when I was a doctoral student at MIT, where he ran the MIT Program on Technology, Business, and the Environment, a program he had started five years prior. He was far ahead of his time. The first business schools did not begin to develop such programs until nearly ten years later, with most starting well after that. But John saw something that few others yet saw, and he built something around that idea when no one else would.

Reflecting on those days, he says, "When I came to MIT in 1986 and wanted to find colleagues to join our embryonic effort in business and environment, we had to build it in the School of Engineering because the School of Management was not really interested. I approached one Sloan Professor who had privately expressed an interest in the environment, and he said, 'John I really would love to do this. I think what you're doing is great. But I can't mention this until I get tenure.' And this was a typical attitude across the spectrum of business schools. Sustainability (though it wasn't called 'sustainability' in those days, it was called 'business and environment') just wasn't an acceptable research and teaching domain in business schools. People would say, 'We teach that in government policy or economics, and we don't need a separate environment and business program.' It's very different today. It has come out of the closet, so to speak, and that's an absolutely essential and critical move. Business schools are now vibrant places where sustainability has become explicit, the commitments are real, and the resources are being provided."

John has always been ahead of the curve on these issues. Beginning in the late 1950s, as a first lieutenant with the U.S. Army Chemical Corps, he was thirty years before the rest of the country in studying chemical contamination at abandoned hazardous waste sites. In 1978 he was chosen by President Jimmy Carter to be chairman of the New England River Basins Commission, a position he held for three years until Ronald Reagan abolished the commission in 1981. After brief stays at Arthur D. Little and Abt Associates, he began teaching at MIT, his alma mater, in 1986 and continued his work until his retirement in 2000.

Today, though retired, John is not retiring. He continues to think deeply, care passionately, and teach energetically, until recently at the Marlboro College Graduate Center and through guest lectures around the world. In 1999, he was honored with a lifetime achievement award from the World Resources Institute; in 2000, he received the Founders Award for Distinguished Service from the Academy of Management; and in 2009 he was awarded the Society Prize from the International Society for Industrial Ecology.

John's legacy is long, and this book is an attempt to capture his work and present it in an uncommon form: as a conversation, one that began in March 2011 when John was asked to give a keynote address at a Sustainability Conference at the Sloan School of Management, MIT. Rather than simply offering prepared remarks, his presentation was in the format of an interview with me. The talk was an unqualified success to all present, and out of it sprang the idea of this book.

To build the narrative in the pages that follow, I merged his ideas—from my two decades of experiences with John, a thorough reading and digesting of his years of blogs, and his book *Sustainability by Design: A Subversive Strategy for Transforming Our Consumer Culture* (Yale University Press, 2008)—into a set of seven discrete segments, which make this book's structure. And then we talked at length. In those taped conversations, we walked our way through his professional life and ideas. What emerged is far more than an academic memoir; out came a manifesto. For John, sustainability is not about windmills, hybrid cars, and green cleaners; it is about the way we live. It is about living authentically; it is about our relationships with nature, with each other, and with ourselves. To be sustainable requires a fundamental shift in our way of thinking and goes to the core of who we are as human beings. Our conversations were about his views on the world as it is, as it is becoming, and what it could be. It is a challenge to us all, and a statement of hope that we can get there.

Andrew J. Hoffman
Ann Arbor, Michigan

FLOURISHING

CHAPTER 1

Introduction

Sustainability has gone "mainstream." Firms develop sustainability strategies, create sustainable products and operations, produce sustainability reports, and appoint "chief sustainability officers" who espouse sustainability to be their core mission. University administrators promote sustainability as central to their curricula. Scholars pursue sustainability as a field of research inquiry. Consumers buy sustainable products, drive sustainable cars, stay at sustainable hotels, and are seemingly bombarded with sustainability marketing campaigns. Indeed, sustainability has reached into all areas of business, politics, and society. The world, it would seem, is on the road to a sustainable future. Or is it?

John Ehrenfeld doesn't think so. And, after thinking, writing, and teaching about sustainability for over twenty years, he has a vantage point from which to make such an indictment. In the words of *Green-Biz* executive editor Joel Makower, "John Ehrenfeld has been pondering sustainability longer and more holistically than most." And John is very concerned about what he sees. While he admits that many good things have come out of our society's pursuit of environmental protection, he sees our efforts as merely a Band-Aid that masks deeper, cultural roots of our sustainability challenge. He writes, "Hybrid cars, LED light bulbs, wind farms, and green buildings, these are all just the trappings that convince us that we are doing something when in fact we are fooling ourselves, and making things worse."

And things are getting worse. According to the UN Millennium Ecosystem Assessment, "Humans have changed Earth's ecosystems more in the past 50 years than in any comparable historical period." We have increased species extinction rates by up to a thousand times over rates typical for Earth's history. Almost 25 percent of the world's most important marine fish stocks are depleted or over-harvested, while 44 percent are fished at their biological limit and vulnerable to collapse. As we extract the world's riches, we contaminate its atmosphere, altering our global climate through the unabated emission of greenhouse gases.

And these impacts are not evenly distributed. According to the UN, the richest 20 percent of the world's population consume over 75 percent of all private goods and services, while the poorest 20 percent consume just 1.5 percent. Of the 4.4 billion people in the developing world (more than half of the world's population), almost 60 percent lack access to safe sewers, 33 percent have no access to clean water, 25 percent lack adequate housing, and 30 percent have no modern health services.

These issues have caught John's attention and his concern. "If a just society is defined by the relationship between the well off and the very poor, we have big trouble. U.S. Census data for 2010 show the widest income gap between rich and poor on record. In 1968, the top 20 percent of Americans had about seven times the income of those living below the poverty line. By 2008, that disparity had grown to about thirteen. By 2010, it had grown to more than fourteen. That the rich get richer while the poor get poorer can seem a timeless cliché, yet something is steadily corroding America. The mythic land of equality has the largest income disparity of any Western nation. How can that be?"

The answer, John finds, lies in who is defining sustainability and what agenda they are pursuing. While the Brundtland Commission Report, *Our Common Future*, popularized "sustainable development" as "development that meets the needs of the present without compromising the ability of future generations to meet their own needs," the concept has been reconstructed by everyone with a stake in the issue: governments, businesses, non-governmental organizations, foundations. You name it, they've used it. But of all these groups, it is perhaps business that has taken the strongest role, embracing the concept as an issue of corporate strategy. And the problem with that, in John's eyes, is that sustainability has become a slave to business interests. It has become merely a label for strategies actually driven by standard economic and institutional mechanisms around efficiency. As a result, sustainability is everywhere, but exists as a demoted and diluted notion, one that is far from its meaningful intent.

CEOs strive to prove "the business case" for sustainability, and in doing so, fit sustainability into the dominant beliefs embedded within the market economy—those very beliefs that caused the problem in the first place. Sustainability in this form is merely a witness to ongoing ecological and social problems without the ability to address the deeply held beliefs that create them. Present-day efforts at sustainability, and indeed society's foundational values themselves, have been corrupted and subverted by utilitarian values that turn them into a marketing pitch. In drifting toward unsustainability, we have lost our vision, and efforts at correction do not go far enough. John writes, "*Sustainability* still has not entered our consciousness in spite of the torrent of its use and that of its distant cousin, *green*. The world of business and government moves merrily along selling its meager efforts as sustainability, avoiding any meaningful appreciation of the fundamental problem or any actions that would make a difference."

"Sustainability still has not entered our consciousness in spite of the torrent of its use and that of its distant cousin, green."

And without that meaningful appreciation, John's greatest concern is complacency. "Far worse than sustainability becoming fashionable is sustainability losing its meaning. Our attention-addled culture has moved on; the topic no longer has the urgency, or at least the headlines, that it did several years ago. This has no correlation whatsoever to things being better by any set of data. It's just that there seems to be a bit of sustainability fatigue out there."

To John, sustainability is not some new "green" technology, triple bottom line metric, or series of strategies for corporations or consumers to adopt. John looks beyond the economic or technological aspects of sustainability and focuses instead on its behavioral, cultural, and institutional underpinnings. In fact, he is skeptical of "sustainable technology" and "sustainable products" as often fooling us into thinking we are solving the problem, when in fact we may be making the problem worse. In his words, "If we learn to make a product or service more sustainable, all we've probably done is figured out how to make the wrong thing last for a longer time. What we need to learn is to make not just any thing, but the right thing, and make it to last for as long as possible." To him, most of our efforts to address sustainability are focused on reducing unsustainability, which is not the same as creating sustainability.

If we are going to address sustainability fully and meaningfully, John explains that we must make fundamental shifts in the way we think and the way we organize our society. What's needed is a deep shift in values that is on a par with the Reformation, the Renaissance, the Enlightenment, or the Industrial Revolution. These are "paradigm shifts" (in the words of philosopher Thomas Kuhn), changes in the way we think about ourselves, each other, and the world around us. In short, sustainability takes a movement to reexamine who we are, why we are here, and how we are connected to everything around us. It's really that big a change, and any change that is short of that scale will not solve the problems we face. The transformation must be based on a recognition that the old way of thinking no longer works; otherwise it will not solve the problems that it has created.

It would appear that an awareness of this failure in our ways of thinking is growing, as systemic breakdowns in mainstream institutions of society become visible: BP's massive oil spill in the Gulf of Mexico; Royal Dutch Shell's dealings with the repressive Nigerian regime; Nike subcontractors' labor practices that approached slavery; Walmart's practices of sexual discrimination, low wages, damage to local economies, and inadequate health care; Coca-Cola's over-use and contamination of groundwater in India; and corporate governance failures at WorldCom, Arthur Andersen, Enron, and the many banks at the center of the 2008 financial crisis. In the face of this growing litany of problems, innumerable people are advocating change; the Occupy protests, the Tea Party, and the Arab Spring are all manifestations of societal frustration with the status quo. They are calls for sustainability in its truest sense.

How does John reach such a conclusion? He reads, he writes, he thinks, and he experiences the world around him; all very deeply. To build his ideas, John uses a complex and imaginative blend of a multitude of voices. As the late Ray Anderson, founder and chairman of pioneering green company Interface, Inc., described him, "Drawing from the works of other giants, and adding his own deep insights, John Ehrenfeld has lit the path that can lead humankind away from the yawning abyss that lies so close before us, toward a wholly appealing goal: an ethical human relationship with Nature and technology." At times John is meditative and reflective, quoting poets and writers such as Emerson, Shakespeare, Steinbeck, Blake, and Whitman. At other times, he is philosophical and academic, drawing from the works of Heidegger, Maslow, Jung, Fromm, and Maturana. And still further, he can be inspirational and hopeful, drawing spiritual support from the writings of Gandhi, Leopold, and Thoreau.

As he puts it all together, John calls for transformational or "subversive" change in the foundational structures of our society. He is highly critical of modern culture, and most critical of the marketplace becoming our central orienting structure, one that promotes an imbalance and disharmony with the world he so deeply cares about. We have become, in John's eyes, a "culture of commerce," in which consuming has become a central tenet of our lives; in fact, for many, the very purpose of their lives. But to John, this path to personal satisfaction is a mirage, an unfulfilled promise, and an unsustainable myth. Recalling organizational scholar William Whyte's *The Organization Man,* John laments a great loss in society as our sense of being and purpose is oriented to our role as consumer and worker. John points out the failure of the predominance of "Economic Man," the archetype of human being that we have adopted, one that is based on measuring value in purely economic terms, sees relationships as primarily transactional, and extols utility (aka wealth) maximization as the ultimate goal in life. "Technology and its marketing, in all its sexiness and allure, feeds our insecurities about who we are and pulls us down the dead-end of feeding that insecurity through further consumption."

John wants us all to recognize that today's society is addicted to certain unsustainable beliefs and practices and that, until we cease the "habitual ways of acting individually and societally," we cannot move toward a sustainable society. He stresses that "sustainability needs to avoid becoming just another thing to measure and manage" and vociferously argues against sustainability ratings of companies and products, mocking the idea that sustainability can be captured by a numerical score, as if this is some kind of contest. For John, it is simply not that simple. The challenge we face in creating sustainability demands a lot more of us as individuals and as a society. It requires, in the words of early twentieth-century ecologist and author of *A Sand County Almanac* Aldo Leopold, an "internal change in our intellectual emphasis, loyalties, affections, and convictions."

Sustainability comes only with a reorientation of our way of thinking. It is about returning to what it means to be human, and pursuing what is truly desirable and satisfying. John's thinking takes us well beyond the tired Brundtland Commission definition of sustainable development, which simply, but more efficiently, continues on the same path of economic development. Instead, he asks us to consider his own, more nuanced definition, which he builds around a rather unusual word: *flourishing*. Not a word that is in regular use within common discourse, flourishing means not only to grow, but to grow well, to prosper, to thrive, to live to the fullest. It is a dynamic word, representing change and striving, not the static sentiment that is projected by the word *sustainable*. For John, sustainability is not a fixed end state to be achieved but a constant reaching for what it truly means to be a human being living in an interconnected and complex world. It is a desirable future; one built not just on technological and material development but also on cultural, personal, and spiritual growth.

So, John defines sustainability as "the possibility that humans and other life will flourish on the Earth forever." Through this definition, he says that he is "trying to elaborate and elucidate the theoretical and philosophical nature of the issue, something that is missing from the sustainability discussion and, I believe, something that people want." As a result, John does not refer to sustainability per se; he refers to *sustainability-as-flourishing*. This modified term adds a culturally meaningful end to our act of sustaining; we strive for a context in which all life can flourish.

To elaborate his definition, John offers two levels of distinction. The first level is that of the individual, at which sustainability-as-flourishing challenges us to shift from defining ourselves by the materials we possess—a mode he calls Having (following the work of German-American humanistic philosopher Erich Fromm)—to defining ourselves by the extent to which we act authentically—a mode he calls Being. Concurrent with that shift is a change in our focus from attending to our Needs to one of attending to our Cares.

The second level is that of the system, at which sustainability-as-flourishing challenges the notions of "rationality" upon which our society is built, but which are practically speaking nothing more than accepted methodologies designed to win arguments, not to find the truthful path forward. John calls us to move away from the pure rationalism of René Descartes and the Enlightenment and toward more balance with pragmatic thinking. As described by people such as nineteenth-century American philosopher William James, if an idea works to explain our experience of the world around us, use it, cultivate it, and allow it to inform our lives until something better comes along.

Consistent with a belief in pragmatism, John builds his ideas by drawing from relevant personal experience and knowledge. "It has always been my opinion that getting involved with the natural world, including a bit of poking and prodding, dirty hands, and new smells is for most people a more intimate and more lasting experience than just looking at it and experiencing it as scenery." To communicate his points more poignantly, he uses personal stories, such as this one about his love for fishing.

> "I always release the stripers, facetiously hoping to catch them a second time. The purported purpose of my fishing is to catch fish, but that's not the real story. I fish to find a quietness, to learn ever more about the world as it exists without human intervention, to sharpen my powers of observation, all of which are difficult to work on in the busy, noisy world I spend most of my life occupying. . . . I believe that fishing involves love. Humberto Maturana, the Chilean biologist and philosopher, claims that love is a basic emotion that determines how humans relate to themselves, others, and the world. The primary feature of love is acceptance of the existence of everything and everybody in the world on their own terms. Love in this way shows up in the world as care. When we love the world, we take care of it, not merely use it. Life requires interacting with it. Fishing brings me closer to the world so that I may discover its essential values and be more care-ful in all of my actions that involve it. Not just the non-built world, but also other people and even myself. Self-love, not the narcissistic kind that is so prevalent today, is an essential foundation for flourishing. It promotes authenticity, and an acute awareness of the interconnection to the web that makes life itself possible."

In ways like this, John both thinks about sustainability and lives it. He tries to use his personal experiences to understand more of the world around him, and in so doing, comes into personal contact with its deeper structures and meaning. Whether he is typing at his desk, casting into a bay along the Maine coast, or working in his garden, it is this affectingly personal experience of sustainability that animates his work. He believes that everyone must find their own personal way to a profound understanding of the natural world and, through it, a deeper understanding of themselves. To make this point, once again he turns to a personal story, this time about the lessons learned from gardening.

> "The gardener plants in the spring and then watches very carefully as the plants sprout, employing understanding gleaned from experience with the garden. Good gardeners know that their plot is unique and that they cannot count entirely on the rules used by the neighbor across the street. Everything they do is contingent. Their methods go into their bag of tricks only if they seem to work, but become suspect when they fail the next time. The theories found in the textbooks at the local agricultural school may serve as starters, but more often than not have only short-lived utility. Good gardeners are pragmatists, not technocrats."

While such vignettes are examples of how John can wax philosophical, he is also impatient and upset. "The once sensitive and dynamic political system in the U.S. has aged badly and suffers from hardening of the arteries," he writes. "The American Dream, always a myth, is no longer even a possibility. Education and access, the enabling structures for upward mobility, are in a sad state of disrepair. The material structures, factories, roads, bridges, public transportation, that facilitate the economics of those that base their livelihood on real work are old and in need of rejuvenation. The financial, entertainment, and sports oligopolies that produce much of the inequality in our society get a disproportionate share of the national wealth, continuing to make matters worse."

In his impatience, John is not afraid to gore some sacred cows of our conventional orthodoxy and find a "third" way. He tries to see beyond the standard bifurcation of debates that are so common in today's binary and partisan thinking. "By keeping within the blinders of their respective ideologies, both the left and the right misunderstand the nature of the problems plaguing this nation and others. The right speaks to the values; the left speaks to the reasoning and rational mind. The right errs more in reducing serious problems to sound bites and solutions based on old worn out bromides. The left errs by pushing policies based on analytically derived programs and expecting to win arguments based on the rational merits of their case. Both are incomplete."

John will also use this kind of thinking to dissect the inconsistencies in himself, those put there by his training, his enculturation in the society of which he is a part but also vigorously criticizes. "I'm not sure which political stance is more precarious: the know-nothings or the rationalists. The danger is that the problems we face are not tractable by either framing. The policies that would emerge from either are constrained by ideologies, although very different ones. Given my history as an engineer and analyst, I should be jumping onto the side of the rationalists, but I am just as uncomfortable there as on the other side." And by breaking down the "old story" that is present in both society and his own thinking, John explores, questions, and ponders the true nature of sustainability as a "new story," both for himself and the world.

In this book, you are invited to come along on an exploration of those old and new stories; to join in a discussion of John Ehrenfeld's ideas, hopes, beliefs, and prescriptions with one of his students, now a professor studying the same topic. The format, as a conversation set in the context of John's past work, is designed to make these ideas accessible and clear. The questions are designed to challenge John to find language that can be appreciated by a wide range of readers. For those looking for a sustainability how-to handbook, you will not find it here. Sustainability needs new and fresh solutions coming from everyday people, not from the usual experts we call on to solve our problems. In this book, we have provided the new ideas necessary to guide those seeking to transform, not just to fix up, our common world.

The book has three parts. We begin with a discourse of the true concept of sustainability as John conceives it and challenging the corporate and technological fixes that we have developed to address it as being at best inadequate and at worst misguided. From there, our conversation makes a transition to John's view of the "new story" that must animate our culture if we are to strive for sustainability; a new way of thinking about who we are and how we fit within the world around us. The book ends with a look to the future; a hopeful discussion of how we will get there from here.

PART I

CLARIFYING THE ISSUE

CHAPTER 2

Sustainability Means Nothing
Without an End in Sight

Sustainability is both a badly misused and abused term. It's misused when those who speak it and act in its name do not understand what it means. It's abused when it is used by agents that know they do not understand it, but use it as an attempt to fool others into thinking that they do. But the word appears to work for both because they are using it as a marketing tool, and we all have become so used to and dependent upon market-based consumption to satisfy our basic human strivings that we have largely forgotten how to live otherwise. We spend so much time on the treadmill of wage work that we have no time left to focus on what we care or should care about. That gap creates suffering which shows up as psychological distress, unfulfilled relationships, disenchantment, and the like. And yet, ironically, we keep seeking fulfillment through that which is moving us further away from it. We have become addicted to all that is blocking sustainability.

The reason this is so, and the reason that the world is in such bad shape, is because our dominant social paradigm no longer fits the world. As long as we operate according to its structure, we will continue to produce unintended consequences that threaten and overwhelm our desired outcomes. We take an action seeking a desired end, and open up a host of problems that we had not foreseen. With each new vista created by innovation comes new understanding of the problems we have created and the new solutions they require. But unintended consequences are often ignored or wished away as merely "side effects." The more the story used to underpin intentional behavior departs from the true and complete understanding of the workings of the world, the larger these undesired results become. Ultimately, the fixes we use to counter their effects are no longer adequate to deal with their size and scope. We need a new story to guide us. In the jargon of social change theory, one might say that we need a new "paradigm," but a "new story" will do for our purposes.

I have been working on issues related to the environment for a long time. But at some point I became convinced that there was something deeply wrong with our culture and the way that our modern industrial society functions, as evidenced by the way that it keeps producing more unsustainability as an unintended consequence. It's not something we want but it keeps showing up. And after a long period of thinking and reflection, something switched in my mind. I began to look at the issue of sustainability from the other side of the mirror, through the looking glass, so to speak. All too often, in the environmentalist's conversation, we speak only in terms of the problems to be solved, and rarely in terms of nurturing possibility. But when we look in the mirror image, something becomes oppositely configured and left becomes right. If one reflected definition of *sustainability* is about fixing present-day problems, the other reflected definition is about creating a positive vision of the future; something we all want. Sustainability, as is presently defined, suffers from this unreflected framing.

For one thing, the way the word is being used suggests a kind of stasis. No self-respecting creative sixteen-year-old is interested in stasis or, for that matter, simply surviving. Sustainability must be a dynamic concept. For another, the most important characteristic of sustainability is that the word, by itself, refers to nothing in particular. It gathers meaning in a practical sense only when that output is named. Sustainability means absolutely nothing in practice without naming the end being sought. This dissonance has serious consequences because it leads to a term that can mean different things to different people depending on the static outcome they seek. It has lost any real meaning.

Stepping away from all this noise, I went back to the dictionary for a proper definition. Sustainability is a generic property of an often complex system describing the capability of that system to continuously produce a desired output. But I struggled for some time to come up with a culturally meaningful property to sustain, one which would meaningfully capture the bundle of ends I identified in my years of work. That's when I settled on *flourishing* as a workable metaphor for the bundle of things that make life worth living and produce well-being. The concept is the antithesis of stasis: a dynamic quality changing as its context changes. It is emergent from the ever-changing world; it appears universally in all cultures, and applies to both individual organisms and collectives: cultures (human) and ecosystems (non-human). I see sustainability as a positive vision and, to refine our thinking, I offer the definition: "sustainability is the possibility that humans and other life will flourish on the Earth forever."

"Sustainability is the possibility that humans and other life will flourish on the Earth forever."

Let's break this definition into its four key elements. First, *flourishing* is the realization of a sense of completeness, independent of our immediate material context. Flourishing is not some permanent state but must be continually generated. The world is always moving forward, and those domains of our lives that have been momentarily satisfied will require attention again and again. But the emptiness associated with our constant striving to "satisfy" insatiable needs is not present. Flourishing is the result of acting out of caring for oneself, other human beings, the rest of the "real, material" world, and also for the out-of-the-world, that is, the spiritual or transcendental world. Attending to these four essential domains of care is what makes us distinctly human. It means tending to family, for example, according to an authentic, self-conscious sense of what matters over time. Completion of one's actions in any domain is not an absolute end, but a state in a never-ending pursuit of flourishing.

Second, it is about *possibility*. Possibility is not a thing. It has no material existence in the world of the present. Possibility is only a word; it means bringing forth from nothingness something we desire to become present. Possibility may be the most powerful word in our language because it enables humans to visualize and strive for a future that is neither available in the present nor may have existed in the past.

Third, the definition includes far more than human benefit. Flourishing pertains to all natural systems that include both *humans and other life*.

Finally, adding *forever* to this definition lends it the timelessness that is found in virtually all conversations about sustainability. In fact, sustainability makes little sense except as a lasting condition. It is that important. For those who would quibble with the use of forever as unrealistic or naïve in the face of evolutionary and geologic changes, its use here is connotative and metaphoric. It means simply that our actions need to take account of the future in a meaningful way, beyond the mere discounting of standard economic calculus.

The central idea of *sustainability-as-flourishing*, then, is a way of capturing many of the individual elements of the problems and solutions that make up the sustainability agenda. I often write sustainability-as-flourishing as a compound noun to emphasize the need to attach a quality to instill explicit meaning. At the root of it, flourishing means more than just remaining healthy. Sustainability-as-flourishing refers to a state of *Being* (a notion that I return to repeatedly in my writing) in which the individual realizes a sense of wholeness, completion, or perfection. The nagging perception of all of one's unaddressed concerns of the world recedes. The positive psychologist, Mihaly Csikszentmihalyi, defines this state as "flow," a condition of "being completely involved in an activity for its own sake. The ego falls away. Time flies. Every action, movement, and thought follows inevitably from the previous one, like playing jazz. Your whole being is involved, and you're using your skills to the utmost." How can we reach this state of flourishing?

The first consideration in answering this question is that this quality is *emergent* from the workings of a system, and only under certain circumstances. The many parts of the system have to be coordinated properly by human agents for the quality to emerge. Nothing can emerge from a mechanical system alone, that is, from a machine. For example, security cannot be produced by technology alone, although it can assist the human agents inevitably involved in the system. So we need to focus on the social systems of which we are a part (our culture) and the natural systems in which we are embedded.

The second consideration is that we need to move to an appreciation that metrics of this system are subjective and qualitative. We need to move away from purely objective, quantitative, and "rational" reasoning to consider the spiritual, experiential, and pragmatic. We, in fact, already do this in some domains of our world. The beauty of a piece of art, for example, is a critical aspect of determining its value in the market or its place in a museum. But, how do we know that quality? We experience and express it.

What I am describing here tells a radically different story than the Brundtland Commission definition of sustainable development. It invokes a different set of characters, seeks a different set of outcomes, and utilizes a different way of thinking. The Brundtland Report offered what has become the iconic definition of sustainable development as "development that meets the needs of the present without compromising the ability of future generations to meet their own needs." This definition is terse but full of moral content as well as real concern for the state of the world. It came out of a concern to do something about climate change, fisheries destruction, habitat destruction, and a host of other pressing problems. The moral core of this statement is equity; making clear that the affluent nations of the world must act to ease and eliminate the poverty rife in much of the world. The report also recognizes the finite capacity of the Earth to support all who are living today and all those who will inhabit the planet in the future. Most simply stated, all have a right to have their needs met.

But the overwhelming central approach of the affluent nations to adhere to the Brundtland definition is to try to hold on to the world as we now have it by doing things better. So in the end, it is fundamentally based on and promotes an eco-efficiency-based argument. Though critically important, this type of approach will not move us toward sustainability. While giving explicit weight to equity and the recognition of limits, this definition of sustainable development rests on the same economics-based paradigm that created the situation it aims to correct. The problem is that we are trying to solve all the apparent problems of unsustainability by using the modernistic frame of thinking and acting that has created the meta-problem of unsustainability in the first place. To paraphrase Albert Einstein, we can't solve problems by using the same kind of thinking we used when we created them.

So in the end, the concept of sustainability is nothing new. It pertains to a generic property of systems to produce something we want over long periods. In looking for a way to attract attention to the environmental and social problems being broadcast to the world, we took up the word sustainability to capture the longings for what has been promised over the ages, and to reflect growing concerns that this goal was endangered. But the word is not enough; its meaning has become diffuse and deflected; it has become jargon describing attempts to follow the same rules, but more efficiently and, to a lesser degree, more equitably. This, per se, is an important goal, but there is no way to ensure that such efforts can be sustained because the underlying cultural structure and the story on which it is based remain unchanged.

We need a new way of describing what we all know. We do share a common future. We should never forget that ultimately our future rests on a healthy planet. We cannot and must not add our own devastation to that which comes from the complexity and unpredictability of the Earth system. We cannot avoid tragedies coming from nature, but we can and must avoid tragedies of our own doing. Sustainability-as-flourishing is a vision that can guide us away from our self-destructive ways.

Andy: What a strange way to close your thoughts. At the beginning you described sustainability as a paradigm shift. But you close by saying that it is nothing new. How do you explain that juxtaposition?

John: Well, I'm really referring to two different things. The concept of sustainability is nothing new, but to actually create it will take a paradigm shift.

A: Is the paradigm shift you describe really on a par with the Reformation, or the Enlightenment?

J: Yes, it's an entirely different way of viewing ourselves and the world than we have had for the last three hundred years or so.

A: Why now? What is it about this particular point in human history that we suddenly need this major shift in the way we think?

J: Although we have been on the cusp of change before, I think there's more concern over the future than we have had for a long time. When people stop being happy and content with things, they start to raise concerns about the future. And today, sustainability is certainly one of those concerns. Further, it's only when the central ideas that drive a society start to fail consistently that people begin to look for new, distinctive ways of thinking and acting.

A: But certainly there are people in the world that are quite happy with their future and others who are not. Is this about more of the discontents expressing their discontent?

J: No. There are certainly a number of people, like myself, who are actively concerned. We see signs of decay in the world and decay in people, many of whom really don't know they are unhappy until they begin to reflect deeply. Increasing numbers of experiments and surveys show that, when asked, people say they are not happy. There are visible signs of breakdown. Almost every social indicator of happiness or well-being has been on the decline for years.

A: When most people talk about sustainability, they talk about it in terms of environmental collapse. You're talking about it in terms of happiness. That's a different angle than I am used to.

J: I talk about it as flourishing. I look at flourishing as a metaphor that captures happiness, health, and the many characteristics of what humans believe is a good life. And it captures a sense of the health of the natural world.

A: Where did you get the word *flourishing*? You say that we really need to frame this as something positive, something we want to strive for, and there are a lot of words you could have chosen. How did you come to hang your ideas on the word flourishing?

J: Well, it just kind of came up. It's really hard for me to pin it down. It was one of those instances where I'd been reaching for a word for some years, but none seemed to work for me. It popped up first during an exercise at a personal training session where I was asked to express an important personal vision. Flourishing captured that vision for me.

A: Were there other words that you toyed with that had similar meaning to *flourishing*?

J: *Thriving, healthy, authentic, whole*—or *wholesome*—come close. But *flourishing* is the most general and historically grounded of all the possible choices. It expresses the beauty of plants and flowers as they develop and unfold. That's the image that is most important. It's the positive image of a world that's working for both humans and everything else. That is critical.

A: Beyond flourishing, you open your definition with the word *possibility*. What do you mean by that? How is that different from probability?

J: *Probability* is always associated with something we think we know; we know enough to predict the future, but we don't know everything, so we leave a little bit to chance. *Possibility* is an entirely different kind of word. Possibility means the creation of something out of nothing. We can talk about paradigm change as really creating new possibilities. We're not so smart as to jump from one paradigm immediately into another and expect it to work the way we want. After all, we have no experience with it. We might consider a desired objective and offer a way to get there, but the world is so complex that there's no guarantee that what we offer is going to work. So therefore, sustainability is simply a possibility that can come as we move forward into a brave new world.

A: Can we take a moment and define some terminology? We have *flourishing*. We also have *sustainable development, sustainable,* and *sustainability*. Can you give some clarity on those latter three terms and how they relate to flourishing?

J: *Sustainable development* refers to conventional economic development as the best way for human beings to move forward, with the proviso that we have to do it more efficiently and fairly. But it's still an economically grounded idea, resting on the notion that the more wealth a nation and the individuals in that nation possess, the better off they are.

Sustainable is an adjective. Sustainable anything is all about the anything; in sustainable development, it's all about development. Sustainable business refers to what the business is going to do to keep itself going. The word is widely misused. The way that businesses and other institutions use the word, it's quite clear that they have no idea of what it is they want to sustain except the status quo.

Sustainability is grammatically and fundamentally different. First of all, it's a noun. It stands by itself, but it doesn't have any normative or social significance. Sustainability, as I already noted, is simply a property of some system to keep producing whatever it is you want. So the key to doing something about sustainability is that you have to first say what you want to sustain. I say that what we want is flourishing. We want the system we live in, Planet Earth, to run in such a way that human beings and all other life are going to flourish. That means that we're not going to have people living so far below the poverty line that they can't subsist, ecosystems will not collapse, and on and on. It's a vision of a world that works. That may sound simplistic, but most people do understand what we mean when we say a world that works.

A: So that's why you talk about sustainability-as-flourishing, not just sustainability. Are you saying that the Brundtland Commission definition is no longer useful, or even misguided? Will it ever get us toward this paradigm shift that you are talking about?

J: No, and it was never intended to. The vision of Brundtland was largely driven by two motivations. The first motivation is recognition that we are overusing the one Earth that we have. Brundtland is trying to help us to live the way we have in the past, but with an appreciation of limits. So it's a call for eco-efficiency, and by and large, that's a good thing in the short term. The second motivation is an explicit awareness of the great disparity in wealth between the North and the South. Equity or fairness is clearly a central thrust of the Brundtland definition. It calls for sharing the Earth's resources more equitably, both in today's world and particularly in tomorrow's world. So by bringing together less harmful material consumption and more equity in the distribution of the wealth of those resources, we have a good temporary approach. But it is not a solution. In the end, we absolutely need to change the fundamental way we live. While it's very important to be more efficient, to reduce impacts, that's not the same as getting us toward sustainability. It's still a system that's running on the old, obsolete engine, but it helps to tune it up until we get a new one.

A: At the center of the Brundtland definition is people. It's about development and satisfying the needs of present and future generations. Nature isn't actually in there. Your definition brings it in explicitly. But let's face some political and religious realities. If people are no longer the center of our defining organizing structure, some people aren't going to go there. Do you see a danger in that? Sustainable development works because it's about development for us. Can we actually remove people from the center of the organizing structures of our society?

J: Flourishing *is* about people too. I'm talking to you as person to person. We speak to one another using language, a human tool. So the human being is central, but the question becomes, "Central to what?" The answer is, "Central to this planet we live on." We're connected to it, and if we ignore it, we do so at our peril. That's one of the basic problems in the Brundtland idea. It is primarily an economic idea, one that casually dismisses the finiteness of the world and our essential interconnections within it.

A: Can we envision a paradigm shift in which people care about the world even if they can't see direct personal benefit?

J: It will be very difficult, but not impossible. There have been cultures in the past that were much more conscious of and attuned to their place in the world. So in many ways, the quest for sustainability-as-flourishing is a quest about going back, not to the same time of course, and not to the same conditions, but to recover a more meaningful sense of ourselves and our way of living within the world. If we see care as a fundamental human trait, then caring for others and the world will become recognized as legitimate, normal, and beneficial actions that add to the possibility of flourishing.

A: I love the way you bring in so many different kinds of poets, philosophers, social theorists, existentialists, and even biologists to your thinking. What are your central inspirations? Where do you get these ideas?

J: I get them from wherever I can, and you're correct that I have drawn on many great minds. I've found it extraordinarily useful to put them together because our notions of culture are a mix of all sorts of ideas, disciplines, and people. If we're going to change our culture toward one that is more sustainable, then we're going to need a large chunk of good thinking. No one person has a monopoly on what it takes to transform the world. So I've gathered these ideas as they fit into the concept of sustainability-as-flourishing. Erich Fromm showed up very early in my work because he writes so clearly about the diminishment of what it is to be human, arguing that we have moved from "Being" creatures to a "Having" mode of existence. The German philosopher Martin Heidegger, although a very controversial figure, deeply probed the notion of what it is to be human, perhaps, more than any other modern thinker. And he stood almost all earlier philosophers on their heads by arguing that Being did not involve some sort of special essence that made our species human, nor was our humanness endowed by a god or some quirk of evolution. Who we are, he said, is determined by the culture we live in; it comes from Being-in-the-world; hyphenated to stress the critical connection to the world in which we are thrust from birth onward. Each human being becomes whomever they are by learning from and existing within a culture that embodies and endows that human being with the knowledge of the world that it takes to live effectively. This, to me, is getting to the essence of sustainability-as-flourishing. To work in that direction, we have to undo the myths that our existing culture is teaching us.

CHAPTER 3

The Myths of Our Modern Culture

The premises around which many of us construct our lives in the modern world are mostly false or obsolete. There is no pot of gold at the end of the rainbow. There may not even be a rainbow if the environment continues to collapse as it has. Novelty and unlimited choice are, even if only passing fancies, full of unintended consequences and hidden harms that erode both the natural world we inhabit and our consciously experienced peace and satisfaction. For a while, I hoped that the vision of sustainable development promoted by the Brundtland Commission and its acolytes might be enough to promote a change in the culture, but now I believe it is completely insufficient. It will take a Jason-like attack to point out the folly (yes, folly) of our ways.

> "There is no pot of gold at the end of the rainbow. There may not even be a rainbow if the environment continues to collapse as it has."

A central problem with our current culture is that the dominant notion of rationality is that of economic man, *Homo economicus*. In this model of thinking, human beings are always attempting to make the most of things, using their resources to maximize their well-being, happiness, pleasure, or whatever word is used to speak about satisfying the self. The self is little more than a bundle of preferences that ebb and flow as they become momentarily satisfied or are pushed aside by another desire that mysteriously pops to the top of the heap. As individuals, we are always presumed to act in our own self-interest, that is, to satisfy our individual needs. Acts that are done for the benefit of others, such as heroism or altruism, are seen as mere manifestations of a certain kind of self-interest in this model, thereby discounting their moral nature. This economic model of rationality does not distinguish among qualitatively different kinds of satisfaction nor does it set any bounds on individual fulfillment. The dominant utilitarian tenor of our and other modern political economies is the maximization of individual and aggregate welfare. The more resources we have to expend and the more we do so, the better off will be the individual "I" and the collective "we."

Consider that in the Depression years of the twentieth century, the predominant national focus was on people, family security, and the risks to the economic well-being that everyone then shared. Now in the twenty-first century, the "people" have all but disappeared. The conversation is now about the federal budget and stock indices, not about the real economy in which real people live. If a moral concept plays a role in today's debates, it is only the stern proselytizing of forcing the government to live within its means. In the discussion of the effects of government policy on the mythical average person, dominant themes are about keeping government out of our lives (and the economy) and allowing individual Americans to fend for themselves. It is about providing incentives for the sick to economize on medical costs and for the already strapped worker to save for retirement.

What is at the root of this thinking? What are the beliefs upon which it is based? Well, if religion boils down to a group's "ultimate concern," then growthism is our religion and the Gross Domestic Product (GDP) is our god. But this religion exacerbates the destructive and violent intrusion of human culture into both nature and our own conceptions of who we are. It is the materialist vision of the "good life" that is so rampant in our culture and so destructive to the environment. It is surely unworthy of free men and women. The fact that religiously oriented people have shown so little interest in questioning such a collapsed spiritual point of view from the perspective of their faith traditions—at least until recently—seems absolutely astounding to me! Greed and its relatives have become reinforced by the beliefs, norms, and institutions of modern economies to the point of appearing fundamental and immanent. Care has been relegated to the "caregivers," professionals who are trained to deliver care to various segments of society. Care is no longer relational, but transactional. The fundamental quality of care that I believe is at the core of human existence has been buried by the same cultural structure that elevates greed. Today, we are living out an American dream that promises a false freedom based on unrestrained choice and the ability to build walls between one's self and the world around us. The life-sustaining power of relationships and strong ties to others has become debilitated by social practices that lessen cultural bonds and destroy community. Our metrics of success are now measured principally in material terms.

But not only have the measures of success in our society changed but also the very terms of a life well lived. For a person who can live within the materialistic illusions of our American dream, the career has to be perfect, the spouse has to be perfect, the children have to be perfect, the home has to be perfect, the car has to be perfect, and the social circle has to be perfect. But hidden behind this idea of perfection is a much-diminished set of values. We agonize a lot over perfection, and we dedicate a lot of time, energy, and money to it—everything from plastic surgery to gated communities of McMansions to the professionalization of our children's activities like soccer and baseball to pricey preschools that prepare four-year-olds for an elite college education. In making ourselves materially rich, we are making ourselves existentially and psychologically poor. This situation is completely unsustainable.

To recognize this folly, we need, among other important qualities of living, to reinterpret our conceptions of poverty. The traditional concept of poverty is limited and restricted, since it refers exclusively to the economic predicaments of people who live below a certain income threshold. Instead, we should speak not of poverty, but of poverties in the manner of the Chilean economist Manfred Max-Neef, who points out that any fundamental human domain of care that lacks adequate resources reveals a kind of poverty. Some examples are poverty of subsistence (due to insufficient income, food, and shelter); of protection (due to bad health systems, violence, and rampant weaponry); of affection (due to authoritarianism, oppression, and exploitative relations); of understanding (due to poor quality of education and media-induced ignorance); of participation (due to marginalization of and discrimination against women, children, and minorities); and of identity (due to imposition of alien values upon local and regional cultures, forced migration, and political exile).

Poverties are not only a description of one's societal or material context. Much more than that, each kind of poverty generates pathologies. Nobel Prize–winning economist Amartya Sen argues that well-being (or flourishing, as I write) requires the availability of a set of basic capabilities such as concern for the distribution of opportunities within society, the importance of real freedoms in the assessment of a person's advantage, an allowance for individual differences in the ability to transform resources into valuable activities, and a balance of materialistic and non-materialistic factors in evaluating human welfare. The huge distance between these capabilities and the way mainstream neoclassical economists view our humanness is the crux of our sustainability challenge. We need to change the way we think about what it means to be human. And to do that, we need to recognize what is getting in the way of that pursuit. We must expose the myths that guide our modern culture.

Consider, for example, the myths that come in the way that science is used to tell stories about the world. The facts that science produces are accepted uncritically—except by those who choose to ignore them or to rely strictly on faith or tenacity for their facts—even as we know deep down that the world is too complex for science to tell us the whole story. Technology, the principal consumer of scientific findings, rests on a foundation of knowledge obtained by examining little parts of that world one at a time. The result is that we know lots about little pieces of the world, but little about the whole system. It follows that technology built on such scientific "facts" will have the same limitations as the models that constrain the designer's technical horizon. While the resultant technological systems will (usually) perform as advertised, they also produce additional outcomes beyond those intended. We may call these "side effects" and try to marginalize them, but they are an inevitable result of the use of technological devices and systems constructed from incomplete conceptions of the world in which they will operate.

Every time you use a technological device, say your smartphone or a light switch, your action is controlled by the designer or engineer's limited model of the world. Sometimes that control is positive; putting on spectacles improves the way the world is viewed by myopic people. But given the inevitable reductionist context for these models, the world that you, the user, are thrust into is often but a shadow of reality. In a sense, any device acts like a filter, shutting out details. Finding your way by using a GPS device eliminates experiencing the real path along which you are traveling as well as a sense of your journey as a whole—something a map cannot convey. The richness that emerges when you are truly present gets diminished. Technology stands between you and the world, and in that separation, something is lost, creating a clear and palpable barrier to our pursuit of sustainability. Technology, as a dominant aspect of our culture, has led us toward a lost sense of the place of humans within and as a part of nature, a lost understanding of what it is to be a human being, and a lost ethical ability to act responsibly. Technology becomes a tool that shields or blinds us from the messiness of human experience and, also, the responsibility for our actions. We have come to believe that technological objects will take care of the "needs" of our own bodies and everything else in the world, relieving us of the responsibility to explicitly reflect on those needs and act accordingly.

And it gets worse with information technology, in which even our most intimate communications become mediated by technology. Though all human (and much animal) life is fundamentally social, the richness and critical functions of relationships get lost through the mindless, unreflective use of "social media." The nature of friendship becomes just another thing we come to "have." Technologies such as Facebook, Linked-In, and Twitter are changing the essence of friendship from the quality of relationships to the simple quantitative measure of how many "friends" one has Internet links to. The important contribution of vital relationships to our Being and, subsequently, our ability to flourish gets lost. Slowly, we become disconnected from the world we would direct toward sustainability.

But it is not only technology that blinds us to the world around us. Every institution of society is based on models and notions of how we believe the world works, and how we believe it should work. Those models become the foundations of our culture, and the myths that rest at its core. Consider the grand pronouncements of neoclassical economics in promoting the utilitarian and materialist visions of prosperity that are endemic to our society. These are myths or, dare I say, untruths. It's not that economics is deliberately hiding the truth; the field is causing accidental misdirection for presenting the results of its models as "truths" that guide policies that have grave societal implications. Lest you think I am being unfair, behavioral economist Paul Farrell, who writes for the far-from-liberal *Wall Street Journal*, took on economics in much stronger words in 2012: "Economics dogma is on track to destroy the world with a misleading ideology . . . [b]ecause all economics is based on the absurd Myth of Perpetual Growth. . . . Economists are master illusionists who rely on a set of fictions, fantasies and forecasts that emanate from a core magical mantra of Perpetual Growth that goes untested year after year." Farrell is part of a growing community of behavioral economists that seeks to alter the stilted models of human behavior that dominate the neoclassical economics field, and its methods for understanding the true nature of the social world.

This community holds out hope that the myths of standard economic models can be changed. But these myths are strong, and perpetuate the dominant notion of the purpose of life as being materially driven and the nature of human interactions as being primarily transactional. The elevated status of the Nobel Prize–winning economists (arguably not true scientists) blinds us to the inevitable unreality in their work. Unlike natural scientists, economists and other social scientists cannot control their experiments, an essential step in providing indisputable "facts" about reality. Their models cannot capture the full complexity of the world and always work in a cloud of uncertainty or, more accurately, ignorance. *Uncertainty* is a nice, neat technical word that means that the information being produced is not precise. Stated more crudely, it means that the models tell lies; little white ones for sure, but untruths about the reality of the systems they apply to.

I belong to a growing community of systems thinkers who see the poor state of the world as the result of a society that believes it is acting rationally when it is acting contrary to its own interests, even its own survival. The British psychiatrist R. D. Laing called this kind of behavior "insanity—a perfectly rational adjustment to the insane world." The reality we claim to perceive exists through the functioning of our cognitive system, which can take on metaphorical images that have been dominated until recently by the idea of a "mind" that the seventeenth-century French philosopher René Descartes popularized. A more modern metaphor is a computer in the head.

In Cartesian thinking we are separate from the world; the evolution of "truths" that form human behavior and consciousness is divided between an external, ahistorical reality and the mind, which through its rational powers re-creates that external world inside the body. Through reductionist scientific reasoning, we view the human being as a mechanistic organism that captures the real world in its mind (knowledge) and operates on that knowledge according to some sort of logical calculus (reason), driving a mental computing machine that's always guiding its actions to produce the most pleasure or utility. The economic model of human beings assumes that this calculus operates to maximize one's desires, utilities, preferences, or some other measure of the priority of satisfaction. In the end, the economic model usually distills utility down to money or material goods because that is easiest to measure and quantify.

This model of the human being is very powerful and has fueled the evolution of the modern era. It began as a means to understand behavior in the market but has bled over to become a central tenet of our social culture as well. And, with such a pervasive spread, it lies at the roots of unsustainability because it leads to an image of insatiability in which human beings are manipulated to convert an in-bred emptiness into unending consumption. Our society of today has built its institutions on this model with the unintended consequence of badly damaging the world we count on for survival and our sense of well-being. But these institutions are slowly being recognized as failing to generate the promise of well-being.

Sustainability-as-flourishing is a vision rising from our present world full of unfulfilled promises. The prolonged absence of satisfactory answers has fueled anger strong enough to ignite bloody revolutions. To create a sustainable world based on flourishing without bloodshed, we need to go straight to our dominant models of rationality and reason. We must recognize that the long evolution of "truths" upon which our culture is built are often merely the arguments made and won by the most powerful members of society. Humberto Maturana tells us that "in the world of objectivity without parentheses [his words for describing the Cartesian system], . . . a claim of knowledge is a demand for obedience." We must remove this invisible, deeply embedded structural cause of domination (power and coercive social norms) in our Western world, but we will still not flourish until we replace it with a new model of what is real and true. Flourishing needs a non-dominating culture to appear.

For centuries, that alternative model was illuminated by the voices of various faiths promising satisfaction in the present or afterlife. The Enlightenment came along with its promise of creating the world of goodness or flourishing through reason. Then came the modern era, merging these promises with a new one that technology and the other fruits of our newfound scientific knowledge would continue the inexorable progress toward human perfection. But problems continue to emerge, and today all is not right with the world. Sustainability is a call to reexamine the foundations of our society once again, and understand and correct the ways in which our modern culture perpetuates the problems it creates. If we are to be effective in setting the world on a trajectory toward sustainability, we have no choice but to be explicitly unreasonable. We must learn and apply a different model of how the world works.

ॐ

Andy: I found the line, "Flourishing needs a non-dominating culture to appear" to be intriguing. But I need it unpacked. Can you clarify a little more of what you are describing?

John: Domination is present in all cultures and represents a great, if not insurmountable, barrier to flourishing; that is, flourishing for everybody. Domination means that you have at least two classes of people that have different opportunities and lives. Domination comes in all parts of the world through authoritarian regimes, religious doctrine, economic structure, and social systems. One area of our present culture in which we have domination is the form of our way of knowing the world. We have this belief in some kind of objective reality that we can come to know through reason. In such a system, as Maturana says, "a claim of knowledge is a demand for obedience." This is so important that I repeat it here. In our present system, we are not allowed to acknowledge two realities. When we see two realities, we're always fighting over them with one believer trying to dominate the other. It's sad to see that this is happening more and more in our political system, but it's a natural outcome of any kind of belief system based on a dominating notion of a fixed, wholly objective world, and the singular truths it produces.

A: John F. Kennedy said, "The great enemy of the truth is very often not the lie—deliberate, contrived, and dishonest—but the myth—persistent, persuasive, and unrealistic. Too often we hold fast to the clichés of our forebears. We subject all facts to a prefabricated set of interpretations. We enjoy the comfort of opinion without the discomfort of thought." Is that the dominating power of culture that you are describing?

J: It all depends on what the culture tells us to think. Our culture is driven by science, by knowledge that's acquired by some form of scientific methodology that produces what we call the "truth." Those who possess the better skills in developing that truth are going to be dominating. I think that Kennedy is speaking more broadly. He is also saying that some things that aren't true hang around long enough that we begin to believe they're true. Those who have been holding those truths will dominate those who don't. This form of domination is very serious because we do not reflect on it and are unaware of how it creates real differences in social power—the ability to coerce people into acting against their own authentic cares.

A: Kennedy closes his quote with, "Mythology distracts us everywhere— in government as in business, in politics as in economics, in foreign affairs as in domestic affairs." In this way, he is identifying places where these myths lie, just as you are. Let's go to some of the myths you point out. First, you devote a good deal of attention toward your discomfort with technology. But I just read environmental author and activist Bill McKibben's *Eaarth*, and my impression is that he sees great hope in technology. He thinks technology is going to save the day. What do you have to say to McKibben?

J: McKibben is very concerned with global warming. It's the central theme in his book and in much of what he's been doing lately. So if you isolate global warming from the other big problems of unsustainability, technology is the primary type of solution being considered; new ways to generate and use energy that eliminate the load on the atmosphere by managing energy more effectively. But I'm talking about technology in a very different way. I have no bone to pick with Bill McKibben or anybody else about the use of technology to deal with our problems; but I also think we need to get to the source of those problems. Technology is a kind of anodyne, a Band-Aid that lets us continue to operate more or less the way we have been without asking ourselves, "Why did we get into this mess in the first place?" Eventually, we need to find out why, and start to address the problems at their roots, not merely treat their symptoms. Technology is always a symptomatic solution. It's always dealing with making some outcome different or better or worse.

A: You talk a lot about unintended consequences and the ways in which technology, which is built on incomplete models of the world, can separate us from reality. Do you feel that technology sometimes takes us on this negativity spiral in which we come up with a new technology, we then discover a problem and instantly turn to develop a new technology to solve it? Will we never stop developing new technologies to solve the problems of past technologies?

J: It's abundantly clear that every technology springs forth from incomplete knowledge of the world. Sometimes that incomplete knowledge is trivial. Sometimes technology works just the way the designer thought it would. But many times what was omitted in the design and conception of that technology turns out to be important. Chlorofluorocarbons (CFCs) are a classic case of finding the dark side too late. When discovered in 1928, they were a wonderful replacement for dangerous and less effective refrigerants; they also created the new market for aerosol products. But some fifty years later, with the discovery of the ozone hole in 1985, we learned that these substances, which were preferable because they were stable, were so stable that they diffuse intact all the way to the stratosphere where they are broken down and destroy the ozone layer. I don't think anybody would have, or could have, predicted this impact at the time. It's just a fact of life that many of our inventions have serious unintended consequences. What's important is how we anticipate this fact. Do we continue to be blind? Do we continue to be always optimistic that every new form of technology is an improvement and pushes us further and further along the axis of progress? Or do we stop now and ask a lot of searching questions before we introduce some of these technologies?

A: A second area toward which you devote some pretty strong language is the field of neoclassical economics. Can I ask you to explain a parenthetical comment in your writing that economists are "arguably not true scientists"?

J: In the truest sense, science is a way of knowing how the world works through a very carefully defined methodology, based on hypotheses, examined under very controlled conditions and subjected to the careful review of the community of their peers. In science, something is true or not depending only on how carefully the methodology was applied. So if you wonder about a true fact, you simply look at how the experiment was done, how the hypotheses were made and proven. Economics isn't a science like that. There is no isolated, controlled laboratory for economics. Its laboratory is the social world, and that world is never the same from moment to moment. The Greek philosopher Heraclitus said that you cannot step in the same river twice. But economics uses models that are based on an unchanging river. They're always based on some arguable assumption under conditions that cannot be controlled. Any application of knowledge that's incomplete but is applied in practice is subject to producing unintended consequences, simply because it doesn't fit the world in the way the designers thought it would.

A: What are some of the unproven assumptions in neoclassical economics that give you the most concern?

J: There's a very clear and careful model on which neoclassical economics has been built; his basic assumption is that humans are maximizing creatures operating out of some kind of mystical utility function. There's also a lot of evidence that this model is invalid, and some economists scramble to try to explain that disconnect. Nobel Prize–winning economist Herbert Simon explained it through his notion of bounded rationality. He said simply that we don't have all the knowledge we think we do so our behavior cannot be predicted as if we are fully rational. That explains everything and leaves a lot unexplained. The part of human behavior that lies outside that which is bounded is extremely significant for understanding our world. It is a helpful improvement, but it still does not lead us to a more accurate picture of reality. Recent work in behavioral economics is encouraging for its attempts to account for broader notions of what it means to be human. But the field still has a long way to go.

A: To me, one of the dangers is not just about economics, but the extent to which economic thinking has permeated our social and political culture. We now live in a commercial society in which the idea of the "pursuit of happiness" has boiled down to "Miller Time" and consuming more stuff. Economic value has trumped most other metrics of value. Why do you think economic measures of material success have had such power to influence our culture?

J: Our social institutions have followed the thinking of economics over a long period of time. But that thinking has changed through the years. Our economy can be traced back to ideas put forward by Adam Smith nearly four hundred years ago—especially the idea of the invisible hand steering the market. His idea of the free market assumed that people will make and buy what they want and that this combination of self-interests will move the economy toward the best of all possible worlds. It is all but forgotten that Smith's model of human nature was based on empathy, not greed or self-interest. But the premise of more modern neoclassical economics has created a structure that is based on consumption and growth. The field of economics has chosen a very narrow definition of what's good for humans based on how wealthy we are and how much income we have.

As the market has slowly swallowed up activities that were delivered on a small scale, it has profoundly affected the culture. The idea of community is vanishing. Steve Marglin, a Harvard economist, wrote a book a few years ago called *The Dismal Science* (a term sometimes used to describe economics) in which he says that the biggest consequence of our economic policies over the past twenty or thirty years has been the loss of community. The big box store is a symbol of what's happening, not only in small, isolated communities but also in the neighborhoods of big cities. The ties that bound people together as we went to the corner store, the local baker, or the local farmer where we bought fresh food every day (as people still do in much of Europe) are all disappearing. The goods that were crafted with concerns for quality are being commoditized and disappearing. The transparency that once existed through commerce is no longer there. When I buy food today, I have no idea how it got to my grocery shelf, what chemicals may have been used, how the environment has been damaged, whether animals were treated humanely, or whether workers were treated fairly. This doesn't have to happen. It is reversible, at least in theory. It's very hard in practice, because these "big" players have become entrenched in the consumerist culture, and have become very powerful.

But we're learning now, hopefully not too late, that material wealth is not the right measure for human well-being. It was an acceptable, effective measure for a while. Very poor people need to have more wealth to subsist, to meet the basic necessities of life, but it doesn't take a lot of income to get to a point where any assessment of happiness has very little to do with increases of some measure of wealth.

A: But certainly this system has worked for many. Over the past hundred years, the world population has increased by a factor of four while GDP has grown by a factor of fourteen and life expectancy has doubled. Isn't this a good thing?

J: Modern capitalism has been progressive, but progressive only on some metrics and without consideration for natural and social limits. Yes, we live longer and (some of us) are healthier. We have in theory more time for leisure, but mostly in theory. Our growing economy comes with a cost that's now so noticeable that many troubling questions have arisen. One of the costs is that we're using up the natural capital of the Earth rather than living off its income. While the actual carrying capacity of the Earth is subject to much uncertainly, we are now living on about one-and-a-half Planet Earth's worth of resources to serve the needs of our current global population. Obviously and necessarily, that cannot continue. Social pathologies are also growing. People are not as happy as our level of affluence would imply. Social breakdowns are growing in kind and magnitude; we have an epidemic of obesity; inequality and barriers to social mobility are widening every year.

Richard Wilkinson and Kate Pickett wrote a book called *The Spirit Level* in which they show that the more unequal a society becomes, the worse it is in terms of life expectancy, infant mortality, health indices, homicide rate, and so on. The correlations are very strong. The worst performer in almost every graph is the United States, which has become the most unequal of all large industrialized nations. So this engine of the modern, technology-based "free market" seems to have hit a limit. I am not saying that it is time to throw it out, but we better darn well begin to examine some of its underlying mechanics and assumptions. We have no choice; physical and material constraints force us to reexamine these assumptions whenever we think about sustainability. Even if we were to be satisfied with the life we lead today, we cannot have it tomorrow when everybody on the planet wants to be like us and is working very hard to get there. That would require the resources of upwards of five Earths. Obviously we must change the way we live.

A: You said that we had more time for leisure, but you added parenthetically that this was "only in theory." What did you mean by that?

J: Comparatively, people in the U.S. work more hours than almost any other affluent country. We spend our lives working. Technology has made that even more possible by extending our offices into our non-working lives through smartphones, for example. This reality became very clear to me in a recent experience with a class I teach in the Managing for Sustainability program at the Marlboro College Graduate School. One of my classes is about organizational change; the students' first assignment was to identify their company's norms and beliefs. One student wrote, "Work equals life." That's nice and simple, but it isn't the kind of belief held by any place where I would choose to work. Now, this is only one company, but I don't think it's an exception. Many employees often work in excess of eight hours a day; they work from their cars and home on evenings and weekends. I was quite a bit stunned by her response.

A: Was this student saying this to affirm or criticize that belief?

J: Both, I think. Work is an important domain of life, but only one of several. One problem in our culture today is that work has become so predominant because we have no boundaries anymore. Work is our identity, both in what we do and in what we buy. When we meet someone new, we ask—"What do you do for a living?" We work to earn money to consume, not to "live." But there is so little real satisfaction to be gained by the commoditized things that are acquired through cold, impersonal market transactions. The encroachment of the market into areas that used to be personal and relational is becoming grotesque. I recently read that you could hire a potty trainer for your child. I mean, what the devil is going on?

A: I once read that there are companies that will decorate your house for Christmas. So I imagined writing a satire about a couple that works all their hours to pay an entire staff to live their lives for them: run their house, raise their children, decorate their house, actually live their entire personal lives! How far do things have to go before that becomes possible?

J: That's not satire, you know; it's already true today.

A: A lot of what you're talking about sounds like what I am or should be hearing in the church, synagogue, temple, or mosque. But I feel that religion has failed to play the role of counterbalance in our society to unrestrained science and rampant materialism. Do you add religion to the myths of our modern culture? Has it failed to provide the human, ethical, or moral point of view to our modern culture?

J: Religion certainly has a role to play because many people's lives are importantly steered by the tenets of their religious faith. But religions, ironically, are not always lined up with sustainability-as-flourishing. For example, some interpretations of our Judeo-Christian heritage have led people to think of themselves as having dominion over the world, using words coming from the Old and New Testaments. Historian Lynn White offered a famous critique in *Science* in 1967, writing that our ecological problems derived from Judeo-Christian attitudes that lead us to think of ourselves as "superior to nature" and to be "contemptuous of it, willing to use it for our slightest whim." This is not sustainable. But in other ways, religion can be a powerful force for committed change and a move away from the materialistic basis of modern life.

A: Are you religious? Does a belief in God guide your thinking?

J: No, I'm an atheist and a modest practitioner of Judaism. I see my religion more as a guide for living. I do this without a belief in God, and that works fine for me and for a lot of other people. I can find spiritual sustenance in my Judaism without the necessity of a transcendent God. My beliefs are all right with my rabbi.

A: I think that it is interesting that you don't believe in God. I do, and we're talking the same language. I resonate with your arguments. It is not dependent on a belief in God to work.

J: What's important to me in religion is not whether the dogma is true or not. The rules for living are the more important draw for me. Do they provide for respect for the earth? Do they hold the earth as sacred, meaning that we should respect and care for it? Do they challenge us not to do violence to it? I'd say most religions leave this out. They are focused mostly on the relations between humans and God, but not with the natural world. There have been some sustainability movements in various religious communities, but they haven't gotten very far. In the end, each religion is a culture complete with its own beliefs, practices, resources, and authority structure. My question is always whether that culture brings us closer to sustainability or further away.

A: We're back to that theme of power and domination.

J: Yes, but these are very old cultures, the oldest cultures. They have left us with an enduring set of beliefs about God and man's relation with the divine, each other, and nature, but they haven't changed much. They've had revolutions and reformations, but by and large religions have stayed culturally very rooted for a long time. So it's difficult to change basic views of the relationships between human beings and the earth, particularly for religions in which the focus had been much more about human relationships with another world. Religions, like all institutions, are hard to change, much harder to change than just about any other, except maybe universities. [laughter]

A: You devote special attention to criticizing Cartesian thinking and the Enlightenment as creating the problems we're running into. Is Descartes really at the root of all this? Do we need to throw his thinking out entirely, or do we need to simply augment his thinking?

J: You never completely throw out an old paradigm. You always build from where you stand, never from a clean slate. Descartes developed and refined the scientific method, but he was building off the work of others, like Galileo and Copernicus. His notion of reductionism and his idea that the world was a machine spawned the technological burst that followed. The more scientific knowledge you have about how the world works, the more stuff you can design with it. So when you discover that the electrons move around the inside of semiconductors, magically the transistor emerges, followed by wonders of modern computation and information technology. It's when Cartesian beliefs and thinking start to become the only way of relating to our world and make our intentions go awry that I become critical.

A: So then, sustainability is not the antithesis of the Enlightenment. It's just the next step building upon the Enlightenment?

J: Yes, it is. We're not going to move away from whatever progress the Enlightenment has brought. There's nothing I say about sustainability-as-flourishing that claims that technology is always bad. I am critical of technology because it sometimes interferes with our well-being, directly and indirectly. The case for technology is never black and white. We need to drop the uncritical optimism that all technological change is good or progressive. The better question is, will the next innovation produce more flourishing than not? Journalist and author Richard Heinberg, who has written extensively on energy, economic, and ecological issues, puts it nicely: "We are living through just the beginning of another [after the Industrial Revolution] transition. . . . Maybe we could call it the Sustainability Revolution, but that might limit it." I beg to differ, this seems to me exactly what we should call what has to happen and soon.

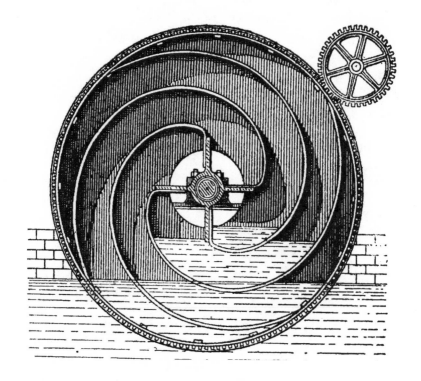

CHAPTER 4

The Wrong-Headed Solutions
of Corporate Sustainability

If you look at the semantics of the phrase "corporate sustainability," it means a condition in which the corporation prospers for a long time. I don't think this is what it was meant to refer to, but there it is. It's important to get this straight because so many businesses (and the business schools that serve them) are increasing their attention to "sustainability" through both words and deeds. Increasing numbers of firms are adopting a program of "corporate sustainability," complete with a "chief sustainability officer," annual sustainability reports, green product lines, and a well-equipped PR department to "sell" them. It is encouraging to see firms show that they are thinking about sustainability, but they have got it mostly or completely wrong. My concern is not that this new awareness is the wrong thing to do, but it can, at best, produce only incremental Band-Aids. It will not solve the unsustainability problem at its roots; it can, at best, only lessen its impacts.

I sit in front of my computer and scan the news almost every day. I type in *sustainability, green, environmentally friendly*, and a host of other related terms and get hundreds of hits a day. What I see are companies talking about their sustainability strategy, and their sustainable and environmentally friendly products. Well, none of them are talking about sustainability-as-flourishing in any real sense. The advertising may be well intentioned but it's misleading for at least three reasons.

First, sustainability is a property of the whole system in which the firm is situated and is interconnected to many other nodes: other firms, customers, the natural environment, regulators, banks, and so on. What matters to sustainability is the health of that worldly system, not the health of any particular enterprise within it.

Second, Corporate Social Responsibility (CSR), which has become the measure of how businesses care about people and the environment beyond the usual economic factors, is either oxymoronic or hypocritical. The CSR programs at companies such as Walmart, which have a strategy to grow in the name of efficiency and at the expense of local merchants and suppliers, are inconsistent with the vision of sustainability. Such efforts hold humans (the workers) only as instrumental factors of production. They have become interchangeable commodities. Philosopher Immanuel Kant's important moral imperative is completely ignored. He said, "Act in such a way that you treat humanity, whether in your own person or in the person of any other, never merely as a means to an end, but always at the same time as an end." With this consideration missing, it is easy to see why flourishing is struggling to burst forth. Most CSR programs merely balance the harms done in one place with token beneficence in another. The stirring of efforts to replace wealth-driving measures like GDP with human-centered measures offers some hope for improvement, but the power and dominance of economic and monetary measures are too strongly supported by the myths of modern culture to be displaced any time soon.

And third, most of these efforts, notably led by groups such as The World Business Council for Sustainable Development and following the mandate of the Brundtland Commission, are built upon the notion of eco-efficiency as the central organizing principle. It is a central tenet of the economic models used to devise public policy and business strategies. Growth depends on efficiency improvements. But while efficiency drives competition and growth, it is not the right answer for sustainability. Like growth, efficiency cannot be the long-run strategy. There simply isn't enough Earth to allow for continuous growth in material terms; and certainly not if growth adds to, rather than reduces, inequality. So while eco-efficiency is a very broad concept and efforts in its name are critically important, to call it a sustainability strategy is misleading.

It is misleading to the public, it is misleading to customers, but more seriously it is misleading to the companies themselves. They honestly (well, some at least) believe that they're creating a better future. But they never carry any explicit message of what future is being envisioned or how their products will get us there. The promise, whether implicit or explicit in the messages that the consuming public receives, entices them to consume even more. That has become our patriotic duty as President George W. Bush exhorted us after 9/11 in his lead-up to the Iraq War: Go shopping! But the sustainable future implicit in President Bush's message cannot be reached through any sort of splurge; it can only be created through well-informed, purposeful actions by the entire socioeconomic system: consumers, producers, citizens, and politicians.

So what companies really are doing when they promote sustainability is, at best, incremental in scope. At worst, they are creating harm by fooling us into thinking we are solving the problem. Corporate sustainability programs are virtually all based on efforts relative to what they would have done according to business as usual (BAU). I call this business almost as usual (BAAU). Awareness of the unintended consequences of the way they went about their business in the past has not sunk in, though it is being talked about at higher levels in firms than it used to be. The number of books and consultants that tout sustainability as the new way toward profits and market share is enormous. I use the pejorative term *tout* purposely here because I believe that the authors and consultants know (or should know) at some level that the profit part of their spiel may be valid, but the sustainability part is mostly bogus.

One aspect of BAAU toward which I direct particular scorn is the idea that we can distill the "attractive" features of products, companies, schools, and so on into a single "score" that captures the essence of their sustainability. Walmart has announced plans to rate the sustainability aspects of the hundreds of thousands of products it sells. We have green ratings of college campuses (Sierra Club Cool Schools); green MBAs (Beyond Gray Pinstripes, now discontinued); corporations (FTSE4Good; Dow Jones Sustainability Index; *Newsweek*'s 500 greenest big U.S. corporations); and safe, healthy, green, and ethical products (GoodGuide).

The idea of ranking things is an old and frequently useful idea. As to the truthfulness and utility of each scheme, however, the devil is in the details. The outcome of any rating system that combines more than a single factor into a score depends entirely on the arbitrary choice of metrics and the weights used in combining them. To be perfectly honest, *Newsweek* should have labeled their listing as the "Greenest Big Companies in America, based on our subjective combination of three independent organization's scoring of environmental impact (45 percent), green policies (45 percent), and reputation (10 percent), normalized to 100 as the top score, all to sell more magazines." They provide just enough information to allow a careful reader, armed with more detailed data, to try to interpret the ratings. But few people are such careful readers, and so the ratings take on a life of their own.

The components used in the scores, just like the scores themselves, are merely estimates and have little connection to reality. Everything that has gone into the *Newsweek* ranking is arbitrary; from the use of revenue to normalized impact scores to the choice of weighting factors and the use of z-scores. Early twentieth-century English philosopher A. N. Whitehead called this kind of error the "Fallacy of Misplaced Concreteness." Even if the numbers were algebraically correct, the real difference between a score of 98.87 and 98.56 is of no meaningful consequence. It is ingenuous to conceal this arbitrariness behind four significant figures. The tangible result of these scores allows the magazine to sell more issues and some firm to boast about being Number One or Two, as if that meant something special.

But, special to whom? Maybe to the stockholders or some regulatory agency or a prospective employee, but the party with the most interest in the matter is Mother Nature, and her question might be, do these numbers have anything to do with how you are treating me? Maybe in some small way, but not in any way that is directly correlated with how badly our environmental world is faring. Mother Nature cares only about the upset we are causing her, not about the intentions or reputation a company possesses. The environment is affected by the actions we take, not by our good intentions or what people say about us. Green policies are just writing on a piece of paper; they mean little until enacted. More than fifteen years ago, my MIT students found that companies that sign on to voluntary, industry-based regulatory programs show great disparities in how they perform under the programs.

Similarly, reputation can certainly be earned, but it is also created by careful public relations. And I hold particular disdain for the advertising agencies and public relations firms that come up with the empty and misleading rhetoric that these firms use to get out their self-serving messages. Only measures directly related to environmental interactions are meaningful in a static index. Reputation and policies might be helpful in guessing who is likely to rank higher in the future. But, in reality, even the efforts of high-scoring firms to lessen the impact of the goods and services that flood the market can't keep up with their drive to sell ever more of the same goods and services.

Don't read this as meaning that I am opposed to these efforts. They are important. Without them, the velocity at which we are approaching a system collapse would be much higher. It is the suggestion that they have anything to do with sustainability that fires me up. They are part of the fundamental strategy of a liberal, free market economy that always tries to hide from the public the externalities (the unseen, unintended consequences of the economy) tied up with the goods and services that we consume. Whether intentional or not, the road to high profits has always been to push the hidden costs onto the consumers and others. Present-day corporate sustainability strategies do exactly this. They ignore the systemic effects of what they do to produce and market their goods. Further, the way they advertise and publicize their programs lulls the public into believing that the firms are taking care of their future.

No matter how many times someone talks about what they are doing for sustainability—using green, sustainable, or sustainability to describe a new product or new program to inform their customers—

they are still in the world of BAAU. It's different from BAU, but it is not the kind of paradigmatic or transformational shift that is necessary to address health, well-being, community building, interconnectedness, and all the other parts of the vision of sustainability-as-flourishing. At this moment in time, almost everything being done in the name of sustainability entails attempts to reduce unsustainability. But reducing unsustainability, although critical, does not and will not create sustainability.

At the root of the wrong-headed solutions of corporate sustainability is the misplaced belief that the market can work if only we could undo all its various generic market failures, often by giving people perfect information through reporting initiatives and scoring systems. Nonsense! This might work if the Smithian ideal of consumer sovereignty held true in today's lopsided marketplace. Adam Smith, John Maynard Keynes, and Peter Drucker have all said that customer satisfaction is the purpose of production and the overall economy. That may be so in theory, but customers are misled and seduced by advertising. Satisfaction has become equivalent to finding the lowest price at the expense of all other qualities, thanks largely to the dominance of the big box stores. Walmart, for example, limits the choice available to buyers by driving out local merchants. Market purists would say that is how the system is supposed to work, creating economies of scale so that all can benefit by lower costs. But at their core, these efforts absolve both the producers and the consumers of responsibility for damages to both people and the world. And that is a dangerous outcome.

All corporate sustainability is built on a reliance on the market, and the market—the dominant symbol in America today—is fundamentally amoral. Robert Heilbroner, the eminent American economic historian, wrote in 1993, "A general subordination of action to market forces de-

[Handwritten marginal notes:]

Is this referring to only corporations?

"At this moment in time, almost everything being done in the name of sustainability entails attempts to reduce unsustainability. But reducing unsustainability, although critical, does not and will not create sustainability."

Big businesses drive out local smaller ones (through better deals)

The way large businesses come in is unsustainable

motes progress itself from a consciously intended social aim to an un-intended consequence of action, thereby robbing it of moral content." More recently, Michael Sandel in his book *What Money Can't Buy* warns that we have been increasing our reliance on markets to support fundamental aspects of our society in ways that undermine its norms of fairness. "Market fundamentalism," in the words of financier George Soros, glorifies wealth as the symbol of the value of individuals in a new aristocracy. It is based on the idea that the market represents the ultimate in personal choice.

Perhaps half of the U.S. adult population supports freer and freer markets, meaning more and more unbound and unregulated choice, and that any rules that govern this "perfect" market should be generated internally by players in the market. So if asked to explain how we make choices in the market, morally driven or otherwise, it is not surprising to me that our explanations point to some inner, narcissistic sense of feeling good, right, or comfortable. But the solutions to sustainability must recognize interconnectedness to others and to the environment. Our culture of commerce, supported by corporate marketing, government policies, and ever-increasing growth as our religious mantra, will never create sustainability.

Yet the appearance of fault lines is starting to crack the foundations on which our market institutions are built. The inescapable limits of the Earth's resources, long ignored by ever- or over-optimistic economists and the politicians they advise, are showing themselves in increasingly stark behaviors. Recent events (financial collapse, catastrophic industrial "accidents," breakdown of public and political discourse and civility, and emergence of the Occupy Wall Street and Tea Party movements) may be showing us the limits within the global market and political systems themselves. Recognizing the inequity in an American system in which the richest 1 percent owns more wealth than the bottom 90 percent (according to the Economic Policy Institute), people are pushing back and saying that the system is broken. Rising energy costs, that can only get higher as supply diminishes and demand grows, will make the cost of goods more expensive and dampen ultimate consumer demand, the primary driver in most growing economies. With the abyss before us, it is long overdue to let go of the mirage that present-day notions of reducing unsustainability will help us achieve a sustainable world.

Andy: A lot of my students, indeed a lot of the public, view capitalism like it's some kind of law of nature, that there's an absolute form and any kind of alteration (such as regulation) in the purely competitive model is some kind of perversion of capitalism. But at the end of the day capitalism is a man-made set of institutions. We set the rules and we can change the rules. Is there a form of capitalism that can be sustainable?

John: It isn't as if the world started out with capitalism as its only model to design economies. For example, once there were barter economies—an interesting way to think about modifying our present capitalism. We in the United States have built a competitive set of rules that drive out small local providers. And the only basis for doing that is to provide lower prices. We can add rules to lead to what we want out of capitalism, but they are not present in the design of existing institutional structures. People argue, for example, for the relocalization of the provisioning of many goods—food, some local services (remember the corner cobbler)—that involve people-to-people relationships. British economist E. F. Schumacher subtitled his wonderful book, *Small Is Beautiful*, "Economics as If People Mattered." This kind of change can be made without destroying the basic political economic structure of capitalism. Anyway, the idea of a completely "free" market is a myth. There has never been a totally free market; there have always been rules coming from the outside that govern the market. You can't fix prices, you can't collude, you can't bribe. We all accept, but still occasionally break, these rules. Likewise, you should not be able to dump the hidden cost of your unsustainable activities on society.

A: You say "the market has no morality in it." But is that what you are suggesting here, to bring morality into the market?

J: It can't be brought into the market, per se. But it can be brought into the political economy. It can be brought into it by the way we tax things, for example. The market is just a place where people buy and sell things. It's sort of a mythical bazaar. So when we talk about capitalism, we're talking about a lot more than the marketplace, we're talking about all of the rules that govern the productive and consumptive parts of our economy. We can certainly begin to change the rules that control business behavior in the marketplace. We can change the way that their profits are taxed. We can put limits on their size. We can set policies for lower growth that are consistent with the limits of the planet. We can create a capitalist system that's not overusing the Earth, hopefully before we reach some dangerous tipping point.

A: To avoid this tipping point, companies are coming out with sustainability approaches and strategies. But you're critical of them. "The Wrong-Headed Solutions of Corporate Sustainability" is the title of this chapter. Are we digging a deeper hole by investing so much financial and human capital in greening?

J: No, my concerns have always been very carefully qualified. It's simply that they're referring to what they are doing by the wrong name. They are not working toward sustainability. They are putting their investment of capital and human resources toward what you called it, greening. I call it reducing unsustainability. It's all worth doing, but only if it is correctly labeled, and not advertised as an approach toward some positive state of the world.

A: You say that "efforts to lessen the impact of the goods and services that flood the market can't keep up with their drive to sell ever more of the same goods and services." Does that mean that green marketing is, by definition, green-washing? In the final analysis, they're still convincing us to buy more stuff, albeit green stuff.

J: No. I don't think so. Green-washing is pretty specific. It's companies that are advertising products as reducing their impact on the environment when they're not doing that. I think that *environmentally friendly* is a meaningless term—nothing is environmentally friendly, there's always some impact on the environment, whether that occurred as the product was being made, used, or discarded, Green-washing refers to deliberate deception. But regardless, greening doesn't get to the real issue of creating sustainability.

A: Companies don't appreciate the distinction of reducing unsustainability versus creating sustainability. Companies just put it all in the same category, calling what they produce a sustainable, environmentally friendly, or green product. How do we turn this around?

J: To get companies to really change direction in a profound way, such change has to come either from leadership within business or from its customers or other stakeholders. My guess is that it will take some kind of customer wakeup call to the fact that all of this talk about sustainability—sustainable business, sustainable luxury, sustainable whatever it is—doesn't mean what it sounds like. They will have to kick back, stop buying, and use social media to organize and to broadcast their complaints against this kind of messaging from business. A few firms already have the leadership that is making this distinction, but there're so few of them that they're not even making ripples. Jeffrey Hollender, formerly at Seventh Generation, comes to mind. His career at the company was characterized by his constant questioning about doing the right thing rather than tending strictly to the company's bottom line.

Businesses can avoid customer revolt by taking a proactive stance and inviting them into normally private activities. Businesses must learn what people "need" to enable their authentic efforts to care, and shape their offerings accordingly. This would mean inviting a sample of potential customers to open up and express themselves in ways that typical market research does not do. Then, companies can continue their involvement by employing some form of participatory design in which the users are part of the design teams, allowing continuous modification based on real experience. I am suggesting that businesses begin to act more pragmatically, with their decisions based on actual experience rather than on the theories of academics, experts, or consultants. Small firms would have an advantage simply because they are naturally closer to their customers. Replace the books by Philip Kotler, Michael Porter, Peter Drucker, and Jack Welch on the boss's shelf with works by E. F. Schumacher, Tim Kasser, Manfred Max-Neef, and (immodestly) myself.

A: You seem to hold Walmart out for some particular disdain. Are you using Walmart as an archetype, or do you really have an issue with the company itself?

J: Both. Walmart's "sustainability" practices will not produce sustainability as I define it. Their program is quite similar to many other large companies and, in this sense, they're an archetype. But given their hegemonic scale and power, I criticize them as being able to impose their will on their customers, suppliers, and employees. Walmart is not a typical company in the sense that it is a giant that is building itself almost entirely on growth. They do not advertise higher quality; their advertisements are always about lower prices. They are a community killer. They have a bad reputation in the way they treat their employees. They've been the subject of a number of lawsuits by their employees. And, as I noted earlier, they set out a couple years ago on a so-called sustainability strategy, but it really wasn't about sustainability-as-flourishing. It was first a means of greening their own business operations. And then they announced a few years ago that they were creating a sustainability index, a score that they would give to all of their products. The thing that really got me going was that it had nothing to do with sustainability. It was only about reducing unsustainability; about reducing the amount of water they were using, the amount of greenhouse gases they were producing, and so forth.

A: Okay, but what about other companies that do not have the same baggage you tie to Walmart? Can you give other examples of wrong-headed solutions in business?

J: Of course! Green-washing, making false or misleading claims about the environmental or social attributes of products or services, is widespread. One of my favorites to criticize is Fiji water. I think the whole bottled water business is unnecessary. How can anyone justify shipping water to the U.S. from a remote Pacific island? Another is Coca-Cola, a company that is creating a paradox by publicizing their environmentally oriented water management programs while contributing to the growing obesity problem in the U.S. and around the world. The Union of Concerned Scientists recently reported that energy companies like ExxonMobil, ConocoPhillips, and DTE Energy were promoting their sustainability programs while funding research and lobbying efforts opposing action on climate change.

One more. The Glad Products Company ran an ad promoting Earth Day 2012, which read, "It's not good for any business—or the environment—to create products that generate significant waste." There's something very dissonant, even cynical, about this, coming from a company that makes its profits from selling us large quantities of throwaway products.

A: Let's move beyond strategies to consider measurement. What would be some metrics for creating sustainability? If you're going to say that sustainability scores are focused on the wrong thing, what might some metrics be that would focus on the right thing?

J: First of all, sustainability is a systems property. You don't measure sustainability; it's only a possibility. You strive to attain it, to bring it forth. It's either present in the system or it's not. So no single company is going to be able to measure—which is what a metric does—their specific contribution to sustainability. What's important is whether they are promoting a culture of flourishing or not. Are they structuring their company to promote fairness, wellness, equality, ecosystem health, and community cohesion? It is only these kinds of measures that would indicate, and only indicate, that a company is working toward, rather than against, sustainability.

A: I have talked to a number of people who have very different opinions about GoodGuide, the web-based product scoring system. Some see it as fantastic because it allows people to create a relative weighting of the sustainability of specific products. Others say it's terrible because it's giving false precision of the sustainability of those products. Does this epitomize what seems to be your biggest complaint, quantifying what is inherently a qualitative measure?

J: GoodGuide is an index that's based on health, environment, and society. It measures each dimension, according to a discrete set of factors, and combines them into a single index. So if it is advertised as a sustainability index—and I don't think that GoodGuide says that any more on their website—that's just misleading. It certainly can be useful, but those who use it need to be clear about what it is telling them. If you want some safe sunscreen for your child, then GoodGuide can give you scores to tell you which is the better product. But it is very limited in helping consumers make choices about "sustainability." The scores convey a misleading picture of their accuracy by reporting their scores with two significant figures, when they're only good to maybe grossly comparing something that has a score of 8 to another that has a score of 6. Perhaps they should issue letter grades instead; it would at least be more accurate.

A: Then it comes down to a question of the goals of these scoring schemes. I think what you're saying is that they're not necessarily designed with the health of the whole system in which the firm or the product is placed.

J: You can adjust GoodGuide to tell you the ranking of a product along the health axis, the environmental axis, or the society axis. But weighting these three categories into one score is completely subjective. The weights are subjective and idiosyncratic, and most users have no idea how to set the weights. The default is equal weighting of the three factors. There is no rationale for this, except convenience. The Good-Guide users can enter their own weights, but I wonder how many understand the system sufficiently to do this. GoodGuide faces the same fundamental problem in presenting composite scores, as does any similar system.

It will be very interesting to see what happens to GoodGuide now that it has been bought by UL Environment, which was formed out of Underwriters Laboratory, a 118-year-old organization known for its ratings on safety. UL is a trusted source of information and has been extremely effective at getting companies to open up details of their products. Will UL be able to do the same on sustainability that they have done on safety? Time will tell. But they seem committed. They have recently acquired a number of green ratings or certifying organizations: GreenGuard, Terrachoice, eco-INSTITUT, and others. So they may be able to aggregate large volumes of data. But again, it all comes down to how you weight it, and how you report it.

A: I want to shift the subject. Beyond scoring, you are also often critical of consultants, and you're particularly critical of marketing efforts that are trying to promote sustainability. I teach at a business school, and I run an institute on corporate sustainability. These are part and parcel of what we do; we try to work sustainability into the existing core, get it into strategy, marketing, operations, and finance. Are you saying that we are going in the wrong direction too?

J: I can't tell without looking at the program. Are you promoting, as I suspect you are, eco-efficiency or corporate social responsibility? Just don't call it sustainability. There's no problem with what you're doing, it's only what you're calling it.

A: So when my students dream of getting that plum job of chief sustainability officer, is that a mirage?

J: No, it's a real job. But the question is, "What are they going to do in that job?" Are they going to try to change the corporate culture to line up its mission and its norms with a culture of flourishing? Or are they going to work to be highly competitive by making their products less impactful than their competitors? Both are good things to do. I hope they'll take on the former mission but, in either case, their efforts must be carefully and properly labeled.

A: You present this duality of reducing unsustainability versus creating sustainability. But is there a way to lay out a continuum of steps in that direction? Waste minimization, pollution prevention, and eco-efficiency—are these steps along the way? Or is it really just a fundamental paradigm shift to go from reducing unsustainability to creating sustainability?

J: It's a fundamental paradigm shift. It takes an entirely different set of practices to change the basic causal roots from those that are producing the unsustainable state of the world to those that will create sustainability. Let me give you an example. We fought a war in Iraq, and then the war stopped, more or less. And we're in that country now trying to create some kind of stable, lasting peace. Stopping the war didn't create peace as we are envisioning it. It's no different here. Stopping the destruction of the earth isn't going to bring us the sustainability-as-flourishing that we envision.

A: I want to end with one last question. As we look back on the chapter titles in this book so far, one might wonder, are you angry?

J: In general, the answer is no. Anger is not an emotion that I find very effective. More accurately, you can talk about my being indignant and sad. Most companies are doing things that are beneath our dignity. They are perilously and unconsciously destroying my world and everybody else's. I can be deeply, profoundly disappointed with or sad about what I see going on, but I hesitate to say I'm angry.

A: Are you impatient?

J: I'm definitely impatient. I don't have that many years to go, and these issues are getting much more serious every day. I have no expectations that we will see flourishing in my lifetime, but I would like to see some signs that we've changed the trajectory. After all, sustainability-as-flourishing is just a possibility. But until we begin to really believe different things, have different goals, and have different visions, that possibility is fleeting. We need to find a way to move away from the core of our central belief that more money and more material goods will make us happier. I'm just one person, but I spend a lot of my life thinking, talking, and writing about this. And yes, I'm impatient. And if that impatience shows up as looking like anger, well that's quite all right with me.

CHAPTER 5

More Is Not Better

Today, the dominance and power of business dwarf that of government in both scale and scope. Business professionals cannot turn away from the responsibility of taking a more central role in planning for and achieving the broad social and environmental ends that we are now pursuing. Those who continue to argue for an "entirely" free market are ignoring the realities of the now deeply interconnected world and, ostrich-like, put their heads into the sand. More and more businesses are adding sustainability to their strategy for survival in the market. But very few of these businesses have yet to understand the full and complex nature of sustainability and the need to shift our cultural models away from consumption and toward caring relationships as a means to achieve satisfaction. They have to wake up to the fact that *more is not better*!

The reason I say this is that, almost without exception, what firms advertise as their sustainability strategy and set of resultant offerings will not and cannot restore the Earth to a condition that could be called sustainable on any terms. All they are doing is slowing down, maybe, their current burdens compared to the impacts they produced in the past. The disabling element of their strategy is hidden in the implicit goal of growth and a more commanding position in the marketplace. Executives of the firms pushing sustainability are deniers of this reality. They are unaware or purposely ignoring that the global economy is already consuming more than the Earth can provide. No matter what happens in the United States and Europe, the burden will increase as the rapidly growing economies of China, India, and elsewhere strive to attain the same levels that we "enjoy."

But do we "enjoy" our consumer lifestyle? Data on drug abuse, crime, social alienation, and disintegrating communities might suggest otherwise. And yet, we continue to seek satisfaction in having and consuming more stuff. And we measure our success through consumption-based metrics such as GDP, ignoring the social ills that underlie it, and thereby reinforce our unsustainable ways. Consider that the United States has the highest number of prisoners per capita in the world; the largest debt; one of the widest gaps between rich and poor; and a level of social immobility that should be a source of shame amid our global peers. Despite these realities, we persist with the model as it is. The drive to finding individual "growth" through more economic goods can be offset, says Richard Heinberg, by a focus on the quality of our lives. Easy to say; hard to define and achieve. But the shift from quantity to quality is a critical and necessary move in keeping the world from falling into discord and decay. How do we create a society that helps us to achieve that shift? We have to change the economy toward one that is not built on growth as its central premise.

"Sustainability demands that the people of the world stop consuming in the way that we do today."

In short, sustainability demands that the people of the world stop consuming in the way that we do today. The qualification in this last sentence is critical. Consumption is an inevitable consequence of life and of cultural existence for humans. If we stop consuming, we will die like all other creatures. It is not that we consume, but the way we consume that matters. The recent Great Recession has led some to argue that a change is happening, that the reduction of consumption (and the reduction of debt to support that consumption) represents a shift in the American psyche that will last well through the next generation. Though politicians seek to restore the system to the way it was in the "good old days," the question of whether the present recession trends and the drop in consumption will be permanent or temporary remains.

Only time will tell. But the recession does provide us with an opportunity to examine how a different set of values that spawn a recovered understanding of the importance of sustainable relationships, not things, will produce a satisfying life.

Unfortunately, while the desirability of moving to a low- or no-growth economy might be recognized by some world leaders, serious strategies that will necessarily threaten large numbers of existing institutions and personal situations have yet to come forth. Reshaping the economic structure will produce many winners and losers, and will be opposed by those, including politicians, who wield power today. The Occupy and Tea Party Movements notwithstanding, the tea leaves appear to be telling us that the power of the hegemons and plutocrats is going to increase in the future unless some major upset changes the game.

That upset will come only if we correct the underlying beliefs that drive our patterns of consumption in the United States. Many contemporary social scientists are seeking to uncover the roots of those beliefs. American psychologist Tim Kasser ties our consumption beliefs to the dominance of extrinsic values that push us to consume to support our images in a culture in which material signs project who we are. British anthropologist Mary Douglas developed a similar theory arguing that we signal who we are and what we want others to understand through the material goods we own. American sociologist Julie Schor thinks that our unceasing desire for novelty starts a cascade of consumption as we upgrade our surroundings to match the novel purchases we make. American psychologist Abraham Maslow says that we consume to satisfy our basic set of needs, starting with subsistence and safety and then advancing to affiliation and actualization. American psychologist Harry Triandis presents a theory that combines past habits with beliefs, social norms, and our emotional affect. All of these theories, which sustainability scholar Tim Jackson covers quite nicely in his edited volume *Sustained Consumption*, point to different connections between our beliefs about who we are as humans and the material goods we possess. Consumption and accumulation (Having) now define a large part of what it means to be human. But the key question that arises from all of these theories is, how do we change our notions of consumption and their tight connection to personal fulfillment and satisfaction?

To answer this question, we need to rethink our measures of well-being to incorporate a reduction in the multiple poverties I talked about in Chapter 3 (subsistence, protection, affection, understanding, participation, and identity), as well as an increase in the positive qualities of well-being. Present-day national indices are inadequate, as they do not recognize our shared global responsibility for protecting the Earth we all inhabit nor do they consider the ways in which our entire social, political, and economic system is depleting it.

So, for example, as the United States moves away from its consumer-based economy and toward a more investment-and-production-based economy, with rising exports, expanding factories, and more good-paying service jobs, we must ask, "Where are these exports supposed to go?" To another economy on its way toward where we already have been? This might be a way to reduce the social burden that unemployment on a local or national scale brings, but it continues to create unsustainability on the global scale. Further, as China ramps up its production of material goods, it increases its GDP as well as its carbon emissions, but for goods that that are not used by the Chinese people but shipped all around the world for use by others. National economic or carbon accounting measures will not capture the systemwide effects of any one nation's activities. The planet doesn't care which continent produces the stresses that are threatening it. So the real question about whether our consumption-based economy is changing is whether the cultural roots of our society have changed globally. We need a different story to explain how we operate in the world.

ॐ

Andy: For many, the central issue underlying the environmental and sustainability problem is population growth. Many scientists think that the Earth has a maximum carrying capacity of nine to ten billion people.

We're presently at seven billion, and we're going to hit nine billion by 2050 according to the UN. Is that when this message of the physical limits of the Earth is really going to take hold?

John: I don't know if it will take that long. It's very possible that we will hit a bifurcation point in the global climate system, a change that will inundate much of the low-lying parts of this world or create massive stresses on food production areas of the globe long before we have ten billion people on Earth.

A: A lot of the future's population growth is going to take place in the developing world, particularly in China and India. Their citizens desire the kind of consumption levels that Americans have because it is so alluring. They want "more is better." Can we think about sustainability in a way for these people to leapfrog our unsustainable values instead of fully embracing our unsustainable lifestyle?

J: No, we have to lead by example. That's one of the issues that has dogged all attempts at global agreements on greenhouse gas controls. We in the West are pointing fingers and saying that you have to do this or that. The answer from the developing countries is universally and rightly, "No, you go first." I don't see a way around that. We have to make some real changes. But it's not politically realistic for any leader in the West to get up and say, "Yeah I know, we'll slow down." They would last for about a day in office, if that long.

A: I've heard all kinds of wild numbers on how much we are consuming, from one-and-a-half Earths up to as many as seven Earths if everyone lived the American lifestyle. But I once used this line of reasoning in a seminar at MIT, and a professor from South America pushed back, charging that this statement is inherently racist because people in the developed world are never going to give up what they have. So then, the only other plausible conclusion is that people in the developing world can't develop. I said that in 1995, and I've never repeated it in a talk since.

J: On the face of it, that's true. If you have a limited resource, and it's being unequally utilized, and you believe the limits are real and have to be accounted for, then simple math would say there has to be some kind of shift from those who have to those who have not. But the prevailing belief that I am what I own stands firmly in the way of any sort of redistribution. We need to break that association in order for people to live more sustainably.

A: Beyond simple consumption, inequality is also becoming increasingly dire. Here are two statistics from the UN that I've always found jaw dropping. The first is that the three richest people in the world have assets that exceed the combined gross domestic product of the forty-eight least-developed countries. The second is that the richest 20 percent of the world's population consume 86 percent of all goods and services while the poorest 20 percent consume just 1.3 percent. And let's own up to it; we are the 20 percent that are consuming 80 percent of the world's goods and services. That's not sustainable. But how do we get ourselves to give up what we have?

J: That is the Gordian Knot. The world has to come together, recognize a common problem, and make a decision in concert that we need to change things. We need to do this together, slowly and transparently, so that the richest 20 percent will understand and support the necessity of some kind of redistribution. People aren't going to accept this without a struggle, although some already do. Some of the wealthiest people in this world are putting their money toward creating the kind of lasting peace in which flourishing can come forth. Billionaires Warren Buffet and Bill Gates have allocated a great deal of their wealth to addressing global problems of inequality. Foundations are doing it too. For example, the Carnegie Foundation is dedicated to the creation of peace. And when this doesn't happen from the top, people will take charge by themselves. That's what happened in the Middle East. When the distribution of well-being is so badly skewed, it is patently unsustainable, and, one way or another, a correction eventually will take place. It came as a revolution in the Middle East. We think that we're not subject to this abrupt change mechanism in the Democratic West, but who knows. I'm not a revolutionary. I am devoted to trying to move toward sustainability without the notion of (bloody) revolution. But something has to happen.

A: A central theme here is that we need to move to a low-, or preferably, no-growth economy. Should we be thinking about ways to get people to stop consuming? Is that a fool's errand?

J: Consumption is an essential part of life. Amoebas consume. All life consumes. So it's not helpful to think about how to stop consumption. That is a fool's errand. It's about how we consume. Why do we choose the things we buy? What do we do with all those goods and services? How does consumption affect our own sense of self? That's what's important. It's not just that consumption places material stresses on the world. We're consuming at a rate of more than one planet. That's a material issue. But it's also that the way we consume has a lot to do with who we are. How do we view the human psyche? Are we really happy? Are we flourishing? Can we flourish in an economic system in which consumption has lost its essential connection to living?

A: For the sake of argument, I'd like to push back and say that we can't change the values that drive our ways of consumption. Or, we can simply say we don't care if people get it. All we can change is behavior. So we could limit the choices we have so that we can only consume in ways that are sustainable. Isn't it more realistic to change behavior than change beliefs?

J: Externally imposed behavior change is going to help, but what needs to happen is much more cultural. It takes a long time for the beliefs driving the new habits to work down into the cultural structure. Only then do the new ways become the accepted routines. Our present culture tells us every day in many different ways that we are and need to be consumers; what we own are our status symbols; we consume to keep up with the Joneses. We have so much productive capacity that it's become essential to market ever more consumer goods. Innovation is sold as something wonderful. Whether it is or is not "wonderful," people "need" the next generation iPad. There are households with iPads that are sitting in a bottom drawer simply because someone wants to show off the latest one sitting on the countertop.

Some people dismiss this behavior glibly as just "human nature," so there is nothing much we can do about it. I don't believe this. But this behavior is so embedded in our culture of materialism that it appears to be human nature, and, therefore, unassailable. If it really is, I think we're pretty well gonzo because we'll get to ten billion people, all living like we are, and then realize that there are not enough planetary resources to live that way. But that doesn't have to happen. We need to recognize that the way we consume does not derive from a fundamental human characteristic. It is a cultural phenomenon. Once we realize that, then we can begin to change it.

A: I often wonder how we will behave in the face of a collective crisis. That is when we will discover the true depths of our culture. Do we exhibit selfish and competitive behavior, or do we exhibit altruistic and collective behavior. After 9/11, the stories of very beautiful cooperation around the country were inspiring. A collective crisis brought out the best in us, at least for a short time. But if we hit ten billion people, and resource scarcity becomes a real issue, what will be the predominant response? What will our culture tell us to do?

J: The emergence of leadership is critical in such circumstances. Modern India was shaped by Mahatma Gandhi, who argued for cooperation and moderation. But the great nations of the world have been much more competitive than cooperative in history. War has been the primary way to settle differences, not some amity pact. Unfortunately, this is the rule not the exception. But aside from this cultural history, the authentic ontology, the way of Being for humans is caring.

A: You talk about a number of theories of why we consume, all based on the idea that there's a connection between who we are as human beings and the material goods we possess. In the most crass form, it's "He who dies with the most toys wins." But that's just a bumper sticker. Sustainability really does come down to redefining how we define ourselves. Is the central dimension here one of turning inward rather than outward for the definition of ourselves and our needs and cares?

J: I'm hesitant to talk about some inner state because I really am not convinced that anything like that exists. But I do think we have an appreciation of wholeness that we experience when we are taking care of our world. That world would include my family, friends, co-workers, community, and the surrounding world. To be human is all about taking care of all these domains. It isn't a measure of how much money I've spent. We need to return to—and *return* is the word I use—a more original, primal sense of what it is to be human.

A: You are critical of using GDP as a measure of well-being. Are there any metrics that we might use as a measure of human progress and flourishing?

J: The problem with GDP is that it's only a measure of the value of goods and services traded in the market. It is not a metric dealing with true human well-being. There is a tacit assumption that the more money and wealth we have, the better off we are. That's been proven wrong. French ex-president Nicolas Sarkozy created a commission, headed by two Nobelists, Joseph Stieglitz and Amartya Sen, that was charged to come up with alternatives to GDP. The report was a very careful and professional critique that recommended a shift in economic emphasis from simply the production of goods to a broader measure of overall well-being, which would include measures for categories such as health, education, and security. It also called for greater focus on the societal effects of income inequality, new ways to measure the economic impact of sustainability (climate change and the like), and recommended ways to include the value of wealth to be passed on to the next generation in today's economic conversations. Similarly, the King of Bhutan has developed another interesting example called Gross National Happiness, which is a composite of indicators that are much more directly related to human well-being than monetary measures. We can create others. We can make up an index of longevity, child education, social mobility, gender equity, and the like; better social metrics of how we, as real, breathing people measure the value of a quality life. It's only a matter of convenience that the field of economics uses money because it's so easy to measure.

A: Bringing this part of our conversation to a close, I hear two parts to your "new story"—sustainability as a trait within the individual and within the system. How do you delineate the two?

J: As long as we have a materialistically defined identity, we will consume insatiably—addicted to consumption. Any sense that there are limits will not matter. A drug addict wants more, always. It doesn't make any difference if his body is falling apart. So flourishing doesn't exist in that world, and sustainability is not possible. If we change our way of talking about ourselves as human beings, then we may move into a system in which flourishing is possible. Sustainability refers only to the system, but flourishing shows up in all the individual parts.

A: Doesn't the arrow go the other way too? Individual flourishing cannot happen without a system in which that individual resides, one that fosters the kind of cultural identity and beliefs about what it means to be human?

J: Yes, we reflect our culture. There's no Freudian ego that lives inside us from birth and is shaped strictly by toilet training and other experiences as an infant. We create an identity as we live in the world culture. So if a culture is telling us that the more goods we have, then the bigger, larger, more powerful, or sexier person we are going to be, we are going to create a consumption-driven economy. If we live in a culture that says the quality of a person's life is reflected in how well we take care of others, the world and themselves, then we will have an entirely different kind of culture that is aligned with sustainability. British sociologist Anthony Giddens speaks of structuration, in which the structure of a culture creates routine behavior; in return, behavior embeds the structure of culture more deeply. So cultures are constituted by a sort of circular process that makes it meaningless to identify either the chicken or the egg as the driver. And in that sense, our "new story" for sustainability-as-flourishing must attend to both the individual and the system.

PART II

LIVING WITH A DIFFERENT STORY

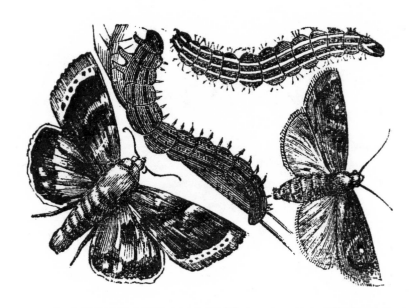

CHAPTER 6

Reexamining What It Means to Be Human

Let's take a moment to recap where we've been. I've defined sustainability around the notion of flourishing forever; I've pointed to the ways in which the "story" of our modern culture has led us away from that direction; I've discussed how efforts at "corporate sustainability" are based on perpetuating that cultural model and are therefore misguided; and I have challenged you to consider why "more is not better" and that we need to change the way we consume.

Now, I want to pull all that together to suggest that we need a "new story," one that helps us to achieve the full possibility of flourishing. The story that individuals and collectives live by is only the plot. The way the plot becomes realized in practice depends on the individual actors—the way they interpret the story in their immediate context. That means that any solutions and how-to's I offer are not particularly special, and would not be likely to fit into any specific context. This part of our conversation is designed to focus on the new story line, to tweak our thinking, and to enable us to design the solutions that can create sustainability. After reading this chapter, you may see that canned solutions to our persistent, most challenging problems are usually part of the problem, not the solution.

I want to tell this story in two parts. In this chapter, I challenge you to reexamine what it means to be human, asking how we can redefine our notions of consumption and derive authentic satisfaction and meaning. In the next chapter, I want to challenge you to reconsider our place within the whole of nature. So this first part is about the individual, and the second part is about the system of which we are a part.

Let me begin with a fairly simple question that I am often asked: "What is 'normal' sustainable consumption?" This question comes from the notion that there is some level of consumption that is both consistent with sustainability and with accepted societal norms. Many approach the question by asking for the consumption level that matches the carrying capacity of the Earth (a monumental measurement task if it can be accomplished at all). But this is the wrong question to ask. We really do not have a clue as to what normal or sustainable consumption "should" be. We know that consumption must be much less than it is today. Sooner or later we are going to have to return to a footprint that matches the one Earth we inhabit.

In utter disregard of that fact, consumption will continue to combine basic subsistence and authentic care for our concerns with the much larger inauthentic overconsumption generated by pressures from the powerful voices of our culture. Those voices can be damped down, but will not disappear. If we continue to advertise the wonders of this or that product (as I am certain we will do for a long time), it will be normal to respond by purchasing ever more. If our dominant values remain extrinsic, focused on how we show up in the world, we will always be trying to catch up with the celebrities of the moment. The thought that normal can be defined otherwise fails to see the interrelationship between societal norms and our desire to consume. This is not just a technical question.

In the shift to sustainability-as-flourishing, we need to become truly *authentic* in our thoughts and deeds. Authentic in my lexicon relates to motivation and thought. It means not acting mindlessly, conforming to some cultural, peer, or other social norm. It means doing something not because "they" tell me to but, rather, from a free choice related to whatever domain of care is getting attention at the moment. It's exceedingly difficult to detect authenticity in someone else's actions. A hug is still a hug whether it comes from an embedded custom or from an authentic expression of caring. Authenticity comes in the way that a human acts out of care for the world, including themselves, other humans, and the entirety of nature. This mode requires an understanding that one's identity is not some ego that exists solely inside the body, but is formed by the assessments of those that observe how people deliver caring in the world, including caring for the actors themselves. It's an easy, but errone-ous, step to attribute one's routine behaviors to some reified inner entity; the real source lies in the structure of the cognitive system—a structure that has been generated by the repetition of one's everyday habits.

To be truly authentic, to realize the potential of flourishing, we need a shift from a view of ourselves first from one of *Having* to one of *Being*, and second from one of *Needing* to one of *Caring*. By developing a dif-ferent story or paradigm to replace the dominant cultural view of what it means to be human, we can begin to realize the possibility of flour-ishing that I describe. It involves breaking addictions that have been put in place by the existing modern culture and replacing them with an adjusted and amended set of values, beliefs, and behaviors, one that fulfills the broken promises that have left people unsatisfied. Some argue that the existing structure is so strongly situated that it will change only through collapse and catastrophe. I do not believe that (or I might spend my time accumulating more stuff), and also believe that we must at least try to change the existing structure. So, let me take the two components of a shifting sense of self that I describe one at a time.

The first centers on the extent to which we have come to exist in a Having mode, as Erich Fromm wrote, through a cultural view of our-selves that has characterized modernity over the past three hundred years or so. We are what we possess; we do not see our value beyond our acquisitions and accomplishments. But Having is not a fundamental characteristic of our species. We are not creatures with insatiable wants and desires, even though that self-view has been reinforced by our pres-ent consumptive patterns. Truly authentic living comes when one ac-cepts that he or she is rootless, that there is no physical thing or nature that grounds our Being or that we can call on to explain who we are in the world. Being is the most primal characteristic that distinguishes humans from all other species. Being is the basic way we exist in the world and is enacted whenever we exhibit authentic care.

Concurrent with the transformation of our ontological model to Being would come a second shift in our model of human action based on Care, not Need. The difference is critical for sustainability. When we act out of Need, except for the biological requirements of subsistence and maybe the first two tiers in Maslow's hierarchy of needs (physiological and safety), cultural norms are always exerting some influence. We may act authentically even in their presence, but, in line with the theories about consumption I mentioned earlier, most of our routine actions will be based on conformance with these norms. Need is based on a deeply embedded insecurity that is fed by our modern culture telling us that we are incomplete or inadequate unless we acquire whatever thing will fill that artificial hole. The more that choice is propelled by social forces, such as advertising and peer pressure, the less authentic the action will be, the less satisfaction will show up at the root of Being, and the more we will go back to the market to fill the hole that never seems to disappear.

Care as the driver of our actions puts each individual squarely in charge. Everyone is responsible for their actions, which might be described as the result of the myriad choices we make during each daily cycle. Choices and actions coming from our sense of Care are authentic; we own them. Caring is manifest first, in acknowledging that we exist in a world that shapes our meaningful actions. Care reflects a consciousness of our interconnectedness with the world (the web of life) and the historic recognition that well-being depends on acting to keep these relationships in a healthy state. Care underpins the development of effective behavioral habits that keep these relationships satisfied. Caring, interpreted this way, is the fundamental foundation to explain human Being—the experience of living.

Institutions built on this premise will be very different from those of today and, I strongly believe, will grow to underpin the possibility of sustainability-as-flourishing, not continue to diminish and degrade that possibility. When we rediscover who we are, we will live out our lives taking care of a world composed of our own selves, other humans, and everything else. Flourishing is a state when all our cares are being addressed satisfactorily. Caring is not about some affective airy-fairy feeling but refers to actions addressing a set of worldly and non-worldly domains, as we move from one to another whenever we believe that the present situation is satisfactory, at least for the moment.

There was a time in early civilizations when Caring explicitly drove human interactions. In past human communities, not cluttered with the distractions of modernity, actions were directed toward taking care of each other, often because cooperation was the only way to survive. Few technological artifacts stood between people's actions and their intended results. Interactions between people and their surrounding environment were direct. While early human life was certainly hard and precarious, one might say that their way of living was sustainable. But after centuries of evolving, societies have become much more complicated. The original Caring way of human Being has become lost as our involvement with others and the world is now largely mediated through technology and a set of impersonal market transactions. Neglecting important domains of Care has caused the collapse of past societies, as environmental historian Jared Diamond writes in *Collapse*, citing habitat destruction, overexploitation, and other breakdowns. Harvard sociologist Robert Putnam, in *Bowling Alone*, wrote that the disappearance of social relationships—social capital as he termed it—contributes to the rise of societal pathologies in the United States. But today, hubris is blinding us to the possibility of collapse for our restless, seemingly all-powerful culture. Sustainability-as-flourishing depends critically on recovering this consciousness of Care, as this is what makes us unique in the world.

"Hubris is blinding us to the possibility of collapse for our restless, seemingly all-powerful culture."

Unfortunately the present cultural story of what it means to be human diverts us from Caring. We, especially in the United States, have become extremely narcissistic. Everything of importance has to be focused on what it means to me. We do little but take care of our own needs until something looms so large that we cannot but turn attention to it. Then the all-too-common response is to ask, "Why is this happening to me?" What we should be asking is, "Why is this happening to others as part of the entirety of our world?" "What did we do to help create it?" and "What can we do to ease this pain and suffering?" But narcissism makes empathy problematic. Inherent moral feelings that might arise from empathetic relationships are inhibited by the shallowness of social interactions in our modern culture.

The stark reality of the 2011 Fukushima Daiichi nuclear disaster in Japan, for example, was a wakeup call to our interconnectedness, not as another opportunity only to see ourselves in the mythical mirror of the pool that entranced Narcissus but also as a way to see ourselves as sharing "our common future." We do much in regard to delivering human and material resources following catastrophic events, but is it out of conformance to a social expectation or out of an authentic response? The motivation matters to sustainability, in which the recovery of our core of Care is essential to flourishing. One of the most important challenges for sustainability is the redesign of our cultural underpinnings (the structure that shapes habits) such that we will become more conscious of the "success" of our acts and move toward authentic choices when we find ourselves slipping into the unsustainable patterns of addiction and ignoring the root causes.

If we can shift the foundational structures of our culture, the existential consequences show up as *possibility*. There is no guarantee that authenticity will bring about sustainability, but it provides a context in which the possibility of flourishing is present in every moment. Authentic action permits us to respond to situations in a way that is unconstrained by what "they say" is the right thing to do, and enables possibility to emerge. There is no possibility to be found in following the crowd, the essence of inauthenticity. Inauthentic actions may be appropriate at certain moments, but they cannot cope with unfamiliar situations. Inauthenticity erodes reflective capabilities and limits the possibility of adjusting to new understanding and changed circumstances. If, for example, consumption of new goods and services is the standard way of coping, an inauthentic actor will go along even if the circumstances have changed and the results are damaging to him- or herself and to the world.

When you come from some authentic source of Care, possibility is limited only by the reality of the world at hand. You can choose freely who you are and what you will do that is consistent with that role. Such pure free choice is limited only by real, material constraints. You cannot give birth to a baby as a man (unless genetic engineering surprises us). Except in rare circumstances, you cannot get a job as a professor at an elite school unless you obtain the credentials of a PhD. You cannot continue to degrade and deplete the Earth's resources if you want your children to enjoy the same environment you did. And you cannot continue to selfishly widen the income gap between rich and poor if you wish to live in a stable, equitable, and flourishing world.

Authentic individuals act out of Care for themselves, other human beings, the rest of the material world, and also the non-world of spirituality. It means that one is free to choose the actions that create identity and relationships, within those real, material limitations. This freedom comes with the price of anxiety. In a sense, authentic actions take us into a kind of foreign land, a terra incognita. Each authentic act of Caring is not a strictly "rational" act derived from some well-constructed argument. We cannot count on the outcomes to be whatever "we say" they will be. But that is exactly what possibility is all about. At first, possibility may not make sense because, by its very nature, possibility means getting into a world that is new and unfamiliar, where appropriate and effective action is as yet unknown. But the positive result of authenticity is the opening of a space of possibility of new practices to become present for us and for those that would follow the new "leaders." It adds to our sense of aliveness, and the authentic actor is able to lead others along the new path.

This brings me to an appreciation for access to the spiritual or transcendental domain as a very important aspect of sustainability-as-flourishing. Spirituality can refer to an ultimate or immaterial reality; an inner path of meditation, prayer, and contemplation that is intended to develop our spiritual life. Spirituality is often experienced as a source of inspiration or orientation in life. It can encompass belief in experiences of the immanent or transcendent nature of the world that enables us to discover our Being; the deepest values and meanings by which we live. I limit spirituality's meaning to the Care we take for whatever we experience as not being in the material world, and which we cannot explain by reference to what we already know about that world. This domain is especially important to sustainability, as it heightens one's sense for the interconnectedness of Being.

At the center of this notion of interconnection is that of love, and it is here that I wish to end my thoughts for the moment. Love is not a something, but a way of acting that accepts the Being of all others as legitimate. It is not fixed, nor can it be possessed. Can we ever have enough love if we think of love as something we can possess? It's not about getting all hot and bothered in the presence of someone special. Our biological and cultural norms may produce strange responses in the presence of a particular individual that we think are signs of love. These are only cultural phenomena. Love is an emotion that sets the context for all of our actions, and it is very tightly bound to flourishing. Love and Care are interdependent concepts.

Chilean biologist and philosopher Humberto Maturana—someone who has had a large influence on my thinking—writes that we are fundamentally loving animals that have become separated from this basic way of accepting and interacting with the world by the forces of modern cultures. It is these beliefs that lead to a privileged way of acting in which we invariably negate—just the opposite of accept—the social status or existential personhood of others with whom we are engaged. So, to come back to a thought I have raised before, sustainability-as-flourishing rests on a recovered consciousness of our lost sense of what it is to be a human being, our lost sense of our place in the natural world, and our lost sense of responsibility for our actions and our relationships to others. Sustainability-as-flourishing without love is not possible. If we do not operate from love, acceptance, and Care, we will continue to dominate others and the world as we do now, with all the negative consequences we call unsustainability. We might talk only glibly about sustainability, but sustainability would not and could not present itself until our culture becomes transformed to foster love.

Andy: We're really getting to the core of your message now, and it is radical. It's very different from other conversations about sustainability of which I've been a part. How did you get to the idea that the core of sustainability is about reexamining what it means to be human?

John: If I had to pick one influence, it would be Erich Fromm's book *To Have or To Be?* He makes a rather stark distinction between the Having and Being modes of life. Further, he argues that Having has led to many of the pathologies of our modern culture of the past few hundred years or so. I couple that to my own experience and to the ideas of Martin Heidegger, who upset the Cartesian model of human cognition and development with his ontology of Being based on Care. Through these ideas, I could see a way out of our basic problems of unsustainability.

A: This approach is not consistent with the way sustainability has become commercialized and publicized in our society. Sustainability is an LED light bulb, hybrid car or LEED certified green building. It's not about who we are as a species; at least not in any conversations I have heard.

J: The discussion over what it is to be human is still far from being mainstream, but it is starting to show up in public conversations. Psychology, for example, has taken a turn from looking at pathologies to looking at so-called positive psychology. I find it interesting that we're seeing signs of a different causative view of what it is to be human, not just as some machine.

A: When you've presented these arguments to audiences, how do they react? Are they puzzled by your use of philosophical models and language to reframe sustainability around cultural change?

J: Yes. I'm still puzzled. Why shouldn't they be? [laughter] I've been teaching in the world of sustainability-focused MBAs, first at Bainbridge Graduate Institute, and then at Marlboro. I have a chance to talk at length about this with my students. At first they're baffled, but they're very open to these ideas. They accept that it will take a different way of seeing ourselves to get to this positive sense of sustainability. But the world outside is still a challenge and will remain so for a while. It takes time to talk through these ideas, and I rarely have that opportunity to enter deeply into a conversation like this one I am having with you. But I believe, after talking with people for a while, they can get it.

A: You bring in the idea of love, which is not as unheard of as it may seem. The conclusion of *Beyond the Limits* by Donella and Dennis Meadows and Jorgen Randers states, "The sustainability revolution will have to be, above all, a societal transformation that permits the best of human nature, rather than the worst, to be expressed and nurtured. . . . It is difficult to speak of or to practice love, friendship, generosity, understanding, and solidarity within a system whose rules, goals, and information streams are geared for lesser human qualities. . . . Collapse cannot be avoided, if people do not learn to view themselves and others with compassion." That is from a book about system dynamics and mathematical modeling, and yet they're talking about the answer being love. I find it fascinating that you're ending up here as well.

J: There are many paths to the realization that love is the most compelling and universal of all human emotions. But more than the kind of love that is commoditized by Hollywood, I'm talking about love as the acceptance of the legitimacy of other people and other living forms to exist. They have a right to exist that's grounded exactly as mine. Love is all about how you act toward, not just how you think about, the world of humans and non-humans. If something exists for itself, then you treat it for itself. You learn how to take care of it. You learn how to respect it. Love is, in a word, Caring. It's personal. It's about relationships. It's the acceptance that you're related to everything.

A: Let's go deeper into what you write when you talk about Being and not Having—capital letter B, capital letter H—as well as Caring, not Needing—capital C, capital N. For you, this is the essence of being authentic. When I read this, I start to think about the notion of a calling or vocation; making your work, what you do, a truly authentic expression of yourself. Students are open to this message, and society needs it. Are we talking the same thing?

J: To your first point, it's an editorial trick to capitalize these words. I do it to make very clear that I'm talking about a particularly human way of acting, of living. To your second point, we're talking the same thing, but I'm a little concerned about the use of the word *calling*, because it frequently is taken to mean a call from God or a call from other mystical sources. Instead, I am simply talking about an authentic statement of what you want to do with your life. But I find that if it's used properly—and I hear what you're saying, that you're encouraging people to take on Care for something—then that's fine. That's what I think a calling is, a vocation. I use much simpler terms instead. I simply say that's part of one's identity and one's Being. It's about caring for something. And if we say that there are some special things you care about and that you take them as a primary interest in your life, you can say I am called to this, but the calling is always one's own. But it comes down to the notion of Care. It's fundamentally based on Care.

A: I don't think of a vocation or calling as necessarily having to be God-centered. It can be. But in all due respect to mythology and religion writer Joseph Campbell, it's more than about just "following your bliss."

I think it's connecting to a need within society and devoting your life, energies, and passions toward addressing it. It's relational.

J: I agree, except for the point about connecting to a need in society. I don't know what society needs, except to be transformed. Caring is a manifestation of one's recognition and appreciation for the connectedness that we have with the world, which includes our society, family, school, and so on. Satisfaction comes not from some inner feeling, but from an assessment that what you care about is being addressed. Satisfaction occurs in the world, not in one's body.

A: I resonated with your notion that to practice Being you have to authentically choose what you do. When I first read this, I was reminded of the writing of organizational development scholar Herbert Shepard and his 1984 article, "On the Realization of Human Potential: Path with a Heart." In finding your authentic self, he asks, "Are you a cormorant?" A cormorant is a bird that is really good at catching fish. The fisherman knows to put a band around the cormorant's neck, tie a rope to its foot, and throw it into the water. The bird keeps coming up with fish and the fisherman keeps taking them away. The bird is acting by the dictates and for the benefit of another. Similarly, our culture will make you into a cormorant if you don't push back and say, this is who I choose to be. One should be driven by their internal sense of authenticity.

J: Authenticity is accepting that you are a human being; that you exist as a human by virtue of how you care for the world. There are no rules about how you do that. Where do you put your time? Do you spend more time with a family? Or do you spend more time in the woods? If those kinds of allocations of your time and your life are internally generated, then you're not listening to somebody else to decide how to be. That's authentic behavior. It's really defined more by what it isn't than what it is. It's best defined by saying, these are actions and activities that you engage in that are not driven by social pressure or conformism. It's these motivations arising outside that get you into the Having rather than Being way of living. And they often show up as a desire to be liked, a desire to be accepted, and a desire to fit in.

A: You briefly mention leadership, that "the authentic actor is able to lead others along the new path." Does this strand of conversation challenge us to think differently about our notions of leadership?

J: Yes. Leadership is one of the most misunderstood concepts that floats around business, business schools, or any organization. I struggle to find a good definition of leadership, and I don't like almost anything I have read. I do not believe that leadership is some mysterious quality that one is born with or is trained to acquire. Like all of our capabilities, leadership is learned through living. Some people care more about the idea of leadership than spend more time and effort to learn how.

A: We live in a modern society that connects leadership with heroism; charisma; or Type A competitive, aggressive behavior. But it seems to me that what you're describing is someone who's more self-aware, connected, introspective, thoughtful, and less impulsively decisive because they recognize the real complexity of decisions.

J: Yes, the more emergent notions of leadership—like systems thinker Otto Scharmer's *Theory U*—are completely consistent with a more reflective type of leadership. Scharmer says that if somebody can quiet their mind, and touch their whole and authentic self, they're capable of leadership. The tie between that kind of leadership as a way to reach sustainability-as-flourishing is self-evident to me.

A: While business schools are beginning to expand their notions of leadership to include ideas like positive organizational scholarship, I fear that the notion of the heroic, decisive, and individual leader is going to be with us for a good long time.

J: I agree. It's very ingrained. But individual businesses are complex organizations and are not describable by some determinant set of rules, even though strategy theorists like to think they are. What's needed in complex systems isn't positive knowledge, it's understanding. Understanding is not granted automatically to those who have been designated leaders by others or by themselves. Understanding comes from a keen sense of observation and continuous learning about the system in which one lives. There are many examples of business failures that can be attributed to smart-ass leaders who thought they had all the answers, but didn't possess an understanding of the system as it had evolved over years of trial and error. Their views came from a textbook, not actual experience. I'm not trying to belittle management education, because it gives principles that work a lot of the time. But leaders come forth when those kinds of things don't work anymore. If things are running along routinely, and someone is "officially" in charge, that's not usually someone I would call, "A Leader."

A: We need organizational cultures that reward and promote people who can understand systems. But right now, many of my students want to emulate the heroic, decisive, singular, and powerful entrepreneurial leader that everyone will follow. They want to be the next Warren Buffett. Do you see something different?

J: I think that's true, because there have been some idols created—Steve Jobs, Bill Gates, or Mark Zuckerberg—very wealthy entrepreneurs that everyone wants to emulate. But I'll give you an example of a case in which the notions that I am offering have been proven to work. The Toyota Production System is fundamentally built around learning on the job, a form of pragmatic learning. In the earlier days, Toyota talked about quality circles, problem-solving groups that were composed of everybody who had an opportunity to observe what was going on, from the boss to the engineers, riveters, and sweepers. Toyota recognized that there was no privilege in understanding the system. Understanding came through a continuous inquiry process that was initiated with every serious breakdown. This model has been widely imitated. So when you say there is little evidence of change in business, you need to get away from the financial and high-tech worlds. You'll find many other examples of systemic leadership in companies that make things, retailers, or service organizations.

A: A point you make several times is that to become authentic, you must enter "terra incognita" or a "new and unfamiliar world," one where you have to "accept that one is rootless." You describe this sort of valley of discomfort that one has to go through, in order to become authentic. Can you talk more about that?

J: That's a direct connection to my readings of Martin Heidegger, who says that authenticity springs from anxiety in the face of death. He says that only when we accept the notion of loss or death can we make free choices. He calls that authentic living. Others who have followed Heidegger have argued that it's not just death, but it's the loss of identity as you shift from one domain to another. So, if you accept that you have chosen to be a house-builder, and at some point in your life, circumstances take you toward another career path such as being a professor, this choice can be authentic, but it is almost always also painful and anxiety producing. A shift into a world of sustainability-as-flourishing will, at first, be painful because we have to give up the old trappings of a familiar, though unsustainable world and worldview. It is a kind of death.

A: German American psychologist Kurt Lewin writes that the first step in any change process is to "unfreeze," break down the old structures of resistance. Or put more colorfully by scientist Edwin Land, co-founder of the Polaroid Corporation, "The first step in having a new idea is to stop having an old idea." These make it sound easy. But to stop having that old idea, to break down the old structures, to, in your words, "live a new story" is a challenging transition.

J: It is. There are many popular personal development programs that are built on this idea. Before you can start to live in a new story, you have to accept that you have been living in an old story. It's the heart and soul of all twelve-step programs to deal with addiction. You have to acknowledge that you're an addict. You have to listen to the story you live. And only then can you begin to move and change things.

A: But you also say that, "Need is based on a deeply embedded insecurity that is fed by our modern culture to tell us that we are incomplete or inadequate, unless we acquire whatever thing it is at the moment that will fit that artificial hole." I read this to mean that we are living in this world that is making us feel insecure, and yet we're afraid to take that step of discomfort in order to break that addiction.

J: It's very hard. I've spent a lot of time in a few personal development programs, and I doubt this book would have come forth if I hadn't had the personal experience of facing the story I lived and freeing myself (slowly) to live with a new one. It was hard work, and many lack the commitment to do it. The thousands of self-help books that are published every year are bought with some hope that a person can simply just adopt a new story, as Nike counsels, "just do it." They all fail. Literally, they fail because they're unwilling to tell the reader, hey, before you really read beyond Chapter 1, you have to face up to who you are now. But we must also recognize that we not only have to face up to who we are, but we also have to recognize that our cultural surroundings feed our habitual behavior. We cannot change to a new story without changing the surroundings that perpetuate the old story.

This is where corporate sustainability can come in. Companies can do so much more if they begin to rethink their so-called human resources strategies. I say "so called" because humans are more than utilitarian resources and, given the way businesses behave these days, these strategies would be better called "inhuman resources." I hear lots of criticism about the failure of our educational system to produce the kind of employees companies need in a fast-moving, highly technological era. That may be true but it is not the whole story. In complaining about "education" business leaders forget about "learning," the more important process. Learning occurs while doing, that is, working and then reflecting on it. Reflection requires a culture of trust and security, both of which are lacking in today's corporate world, at least at the level of the worker; the senior executives, with their massive salaries and severance packages seem to be doing just fine. While lifetime employment may be outmoded, businesses must provide a more secure and enriching working place. All the math and science education in the world won't provide them the kind of employees that are critical to success in today's flat world unless they also cultivate human potential. Companies claiming to be concerned about sustainability cannot do anything about it until they learn how to care and practice it at home. Only then will they be able to change the world at large through the goods and services they bring to the market. In the end, true corporate sustainability programs must begin with a new story of how they treat and cultivate their employees.

CHAPTER 7

Returning to Our Place in the Whole

The second part of a new story that can lead us to sustainability-as-flourishing is a rewrite of the beliefs by which we conceive of and relate to the natural and social worlds. Our contemporary conversation about sustainability is taking place without a clear understanding, or with purposeful ignorance, of our place within a *complex* world. Complexity refers to a system whose parts are so multiply interconnected that it is impossible to predict how it will behave when perturbed. Complexity is also used to describe systems that can move from chaos to order; that is, they are self-organizing. This means that the converse is also true; complex systems also have the unfortunate possibility of reversing that direction and going from order to chaos, as did the global financial system in 2008.

One cause for the present unsustainable state of the world is our failure to fully recognize the complex nature of the world and act accordingly. We desperately wish to keep our societal machinery running and pouring out everything we need from all the spigots of the economy. That's what most people think about when they use the word *sustainable*. Please keep the machine going so I can keep getting a new iPad every two years! We risk getting what we are asking for—an inauthentic, unsatisfying life of Having, not one of Being. Our culture leads us to this thin view of what life is all about, and so we don't bother to look for the fullness of flourishing. Until we recognize and accept that we humans are an integral part of the complex system we call Earth, the possibility of sustainability will be nil.

We must begin by recognizing and accepting that each one of us is merely a node in an interconnected web of life and that sustainability-as-flourishing is an emergent property of the complex system we inhabit. Understanding this complexity demands a belief about reality that is different from the current objective view of the world, one in which we discover reality through scientific investigations and extend it through theorizing. Our scientific method has led us to believe that we exist outside of that system and can get to know it in the same way that we learn to design and fix an automobile or a washing machine. It is based on a reductionist view of the world: how we come to know it, how we act to realize our intentions, and how we explain why we acted as we did. But this kind of knowledge is always partial and limited to a part or collection of parts of the system. Under these beliefs, truth becomes manifest only in the findings of the scientific method—proving hypotheses through experiments. Stated in the simplest terms, the dominant belief system from which scientific truth emerges is that of the world as a vast machine, governed by analytically describable relationships that we can come to know through normal, objective science. And armed with this knowledge, we can design institutions and technologies that we believe will always move the world in a progressive direction. These rationally derived truths become the basis of claims we make in everyday, normal conversations. They become what the great, early-twentieth-century French sociologist Emile Durkheim calls "social facts," taken-for-granted beliefs that guide our everyday life and that we teach to others as the correct way to think.

But there's a serious problem here. A central feature and barrier in the search for sustainability today is the dominance of this objective, positivist framework. It has produced much "progress" compared to the state of well-being that existed at the time of the Enlightenment. But progress has been measured by sets of generally quantitative, disparate metrics that fail to capture the holistic qualities of life. By other measures, real human progress on a systems scale has not been so great. Flourishing and other similar qualities emerge from the working of the system as a whole and cannot be described by any reductionist set of rules. Try as hard as we can to operate with our present kind of rational reasoning, we are not going to produce sustainability-as-flourishing, except by accident.

We are now beginning to understand that the world is not the (complicated) machine that René Descartes and his followers thought it was. In fact, it is different in such important and fundamental ways that we can say that complexity is part of another paradigm. The Cartesian idea of a mind capturing the information coming via the senses (mirroring nature) and manipulating those images using our rational machinery, has led to an inaccurate picture of the mental system as a sort of computer with a built-in logic, just like the PCs most of us use every day. But neither we, nor the world, are reducible to such a mechanical metaphor. We, and the world, are complex and behave in nonlinear and unpredictable ways. Complexity does not rule out the finding of truths about the world that can be used to design and govern it, but the scientific method cannot be counted upon to generate *all* of the knowledge needed. Our knowledge about the world will always be incomplete. If we accept that, we can adjust and act appropriately. Indeed we must. As the world turns lately, our knowledge-based rules are leading to bigger and bigger failures.

Our dominant mode of *reasoning*, generally seen as a means to improve knowledge and the ways we act upon it, often leads to epistemic distortions and poor decisions. Reasoning is more like a method to make one's point; to devise and evaluate arguments intended to persuade. Skilled, rational arguers often are not after the truth but after "winning" with arguments supporting their views. The "rational" deterministic rules and procedures that form the base for almost all public decisions need to be augmented by pragmatic inquiries that find truth as the successful coping with the vagaries of life on an ever-changing planet. The Cartesian machine no longer follows the rules we impose upon it and is beginning to break down. To achieve sustainability-as-flourishing, we must shift the multiple components of our models of thinking to embrace complexity as the foundation of life. I see three components that need shifting, but I am sure there are more.

The first important component is that the complex Earth system cannot be reduced to a set of analytic rules that both explain and predict its behavior. Future behavior cannot be related to the present and past states of the system with any real certainty using the scientific method alone. Further, the future states may be disconnected from the present and be located in entirely different regimes where behavioral patterns are nothing like those of the previous one. Chaotic situations remain chaotic until something perturbs the system and creates order, but we cannot tell in advance what the ordered system will look like.

A second important component is that the model of learning and knowledge necessary to understand sustainability in a complex system contradicts the conventional Cartesian model of cognition. Complexity study is the antithesis of classical scientific work, which is based on the search for laws that will predict the behavior of various parts of the world. This tension must be very frustrating to many scientists who are not yet ready to drop the scientific method of revealing truth for a method that can only describe behavior in general terms. Complexity is amenable to some analysis; it's possible to understand the basic rules that bring order to a flock of birds, but not to map the actual behavior at any instant. The errant behavior of a single member of the flock can turn the orderly movements back to chaos in an instant.

A third important component is that we must replace the apparent certainty of technocratic designs with adaptive and resilient systems built on understanding that is gained by experience. We are not Cartesian beings with a mind separate from the body for taking in and representing the world. We learn through experiencing the world via the actions we engage in. Humberto Maturana writes, "Learning is doing; doing is learning," as he argues for an alternative form of reasoning based on a reality that is created through a person's life experience and emerges through social interactions. When the subjective world appears the same to many people, it's not because it has some eternal fixed form outside of our consciousness, but because we have been socialized in a common culture and have adopted the same set of basic beliefs and norms in order to perceive it. We have lost a great deal of our capacity to see the world in authentic and personal terms. We see it instead through the myths of our modern culture.

If we are to cope with the huge social and environmental breakdowns of the moment, we have to start by telling the truth, as closely as we can. *Pragmatism*, an important element of leadership for sustainability-as-flourishing, helps us to move toward the direction of that truth. Pragmatism at work couples cognitive models to a criterion for assessing the effectiveness of outcomes obtained by deliberately perturbing a system, that is, inducing changes in the structure. If the system works better relative to its goals, the perturbation was good. If it doesn't, try another modification. By developing an experiential viewpoint from which to understand our world, we find the truth in practice through a continuing inquiry process, and apply it to underpin and explain our successful actions. Truth is then manifest in outcomes that work as desired. Pragmatism is a way of acting deliberately and consciously within the partial truths of scientific analysis, always watching the results and adjusting to maintain the course toward the ends being sought. We seek truth by continually inquiring, experimenting, and acting until we arrive at the end we envisioned: flourishing, in this case.

From all this, it follows that the reality we live depends on the explanatory path we adopt, and this in turn depends on the emotional domain from which we act. Thus, if we are in an assertive and dominating mode and we want to impose our views on another without reflection, de facto negating him or her, we find ourselves operating in the explanatory path of a reality that is created by forcing a person's analytic rules upon the world. This is the standard view. If, on the contrary, we are acting from the domain that accepts the other in the mood of reflection, we return to the explanatory path of a reality that is created through life experience and social interactions. In the end, our reality reflects the flow of our interpersonal relations and the actions we choose to take within them.

In addition to the way we care and behave in the material world, we must also recognize and care for the out-of-the-world domain of spirituality, through which we experience connectedness to the web of life, illuminating our ties to other individuals, with the human community, with nature, and with the cosmos. To counter what another great, early-twentieth-century sociologist Max Weber wrote, "The fate of our times is characterized by rationalization and intellectualization and, above all, by the disenchantment of the world," we have to recover the sense of the sacredness of the world, even of the cosmos, that envelops us.

"We have to recover the sense of the sacredness of the world, even of the cosmos, that envelops us."

Understanding of the complexity of the world must diffuse from the scientists' supercomputers to the everyday thoughts and beliefs of ordinary laypersons. We must learn to live not just through the models and rules of modern society. We must also learn to live through experience with the subjective world in which we live, one in which we are relationally bound. Spirituality is one source of inspiration or orientation in life that helps us see the possibility of flourishing. It can encompass belief in immaterial realities or experiences of the immanent or transcendent nature of the world that help a person to discover the meaning of their Being, and the deepest values by which we can live. Flourishing is nothing more than a state recognized when one says, "All my cares are being satisfied, at least for the moment." The spiritual domain is one of those important domains of Care, but is often overlooked today. Here in this domain, one recognizes, in a deep and profound way, that the narcissistic needs that are directed inwardly are not as powerful or as enriching as the care that is directed outwardly. In the end, we will know the world and act authentically within it only if we adopt a new and more nuanced way of relating to it: complexity, which blends objective elements of the scientific method with the subjective elements of pragmatic, spiritual, and loving Being. Only then can we find our way to sustainability-as-flourishing.

❦

Andy: You devote a major part of this chapter to moving beyond the Cartesian idea of the world as a machine and returning to a sense of the sacred in the world around us. This reminded me of *Death of Nature* by ecofeminist philosopher Carolyn Merchant. She describes our view prior to the Enlightenment as one in which nature was the benevolent mother of all things. She is critical of the Dominion model of the scientific revolution that dissected nature, best exemplified by seventeenth-century English philosopher Francis Bacon's statement that science "tortures nature's secrets out of her." Are you talking about going back to a pre-Enlightenment time or to some new stage that brings us all together in a cohesive whole?

John: I think that "back to the future" is a better statement of where we are. Going back without some qualification sounds like we're giving up. We're going back, in a sense, to a mind-set containing elements that were important in past moments of time. We're never going to go all the way back. We live in a modern world. Our institutions are shaped by technology, technocracy, and scientific principles. We're not instantly going away from them, but we do need to modify and, in some cases, transform them. There is no reason that age-old ideas about what it means to be human cannot be brought back and reinjected into the modern world. We know that we can authentically express our Caring even in the noisy hurly burly of modern life. It's never going to be easy, but we must learn how.

A: Putting this together in a historical trajectory: we have a pre-Enlightenment model of nature as an organic system that is animated by mystical forces; then the Enlightenment teaches us to understand the world as a machine; now we're running into problems that a machine model of the world can't explain. You are saying that we lost something from that pre-Enlightenment period and we're now trying to bring it back into our story to build a more complete picture of the world. But you add an interesting component: we need to "recover this sense of the sacredness of our world." How does this fit into the evolving story?

J: Sacredness falls into one of those domains of Caring that will be difficult, as I just said, to fit into our modern life. But we must do it. Sacredness, for me, represents an enhanced consciousness, one that is based on something connected to spirituality. I define *sacred* without straying into more conventional religious notions. While collectives can offer up the same object or symbol as sacred, only individuals can decide whether or not to accept it as such. Sacred objects are symbols that unite a society, family, or other collective. They produce a personal consciousness of one's connection to the world around you.

If you become conscious of connections to everything, not just the immediate world before you, you will experience a much broader and more powerful sense of Being. Some Native Americans talk about being part of the web of life. They connect everything to everything, and so develop respect for everything as sacred. They learn to run their lives out of that respect in order to keep that whole system intact. It's a much harder job today. Our world is more complicated and full of things than the world of the Native Americans was a few hundred years ago. But the idea is still very powerful and absolutely essential for achieving the systemic outcomes that I associate with sustainability-as-flourishing. Naturalist Rachel Carson reminded us of this need in her book *Silent Spring*. It's been fifty years since she wrote it, and we are still struggling with a way to fit our modern society into the web of life. She didn't reject modern science. She merely pointed out that our scientific method, and what she called "the arrogance of man," has led us to misreading our place within the system of nature. She argued for some humility and respect when our technologies intrude upon nature.

A: So are you saying that spirituality leads to a reconnection to the system, to embracing our place within the whole?

J: Absolutely. One of the most important notions that comes out of appreciating the spiritual domain is that it is grounded on a sense of interconnectedness. Just imagine, for a moment, that the explanations given to spiritual phenomena were often attributed to some kind of mystical force or mystical being. I think that anthropological research bears this out. But taking this one step further, that picture includes some sort of connectedness to what's out there. Spirituality leads to practices in daily living that reflect a sense of connectedness to the world. Sustainability-as-flourishing could come much faster if we moderns would put spirituality back into the place it belongs and deserves.

A: You make a point that complexity study is the antithesis of classical scientific analysis; certainly spirituality is as well. Can we not understand the entirety of the system through science? Are you talking about augmenting or replacing classical scientific approaches to understanding the complexity of the world around us?

J: I think that *complementing* is the right word. Science is powerful. I'm not arguing that we shouldn't be looking at things scientifically, but the methods of science inevitably force us to take the system apart, leaving only pieces that we can control, reproduce, and use to reconstruct the whole system. Once we really start to look at the system as a whole, however, whether it's a human being or the world, it gets to be very difficult to use this method. We begin to realize that it's not just how each part works, it's understanding how they work together. When you get beyond a few pieces with all the ties between them, it becomes mind-boggling. There is just too much out there to reduce to some set of analytic rules. These complex systems do not always behave in nice, linear, predictable ways. Their rules, when we can write them down, are often nonlinear, confounding the usual methods of analysis.

A: I'm still not ready to go all the way with you here. We live in a day when large datasets and powerful computing models allow us to see the complexity of the world in a whole new way. For example, we wouldn't understand climate change if we didn't have very powerful computers that could aggregate all the data into models that help us to understand it. Isn't this kind of analysis going to help in the understanding of complexity you seek?

J: I want the computer's help as a start to understand complexity, but big computers can't produce the whole answer, certainly not if we are looking at global-scale systems. For example, a lot of questions remain about how to connect the sub-models driving climate change. The modelers talk about feedback. Well, feedback is just a technical name for a kind of interconnection. So, even with all of this power of scientists and their tools, we will still be faced with some basic lack of understanding.

We deal with these problems in terms of certainty and probabilities, but that's not what complexity is all about. As former U.S. Secretary of Defense Donald Rumsfeld famously said, "there are unknown unknowns, things we don't know we don't know." We must operate pragmatically, discovering "truth" through a continuing inquiry process. Pragmatic truths are a different kind of beliefs than those resulting from scientific methodology, although the two may appear to be the same. The pragmatic truth works even if you don't know you are leaving something important out. You just keep trying new ideas and assessing the outcomes, until you get to a satisfactory end-point. The last ideas you applied become the pragmatic "truth."

In my own life, I keep trying new ideas and learn from what I do. None are likely to bring down my entire life. When you're mucking around with the whole global system, the ideas you try out are much more consequential. I hear a lot of talk about geo-engineering—playing with the whole Earth system by putting stuff in the ocean to make algae bloom or throwing stuff in the atmosphere to reflect more of the sun's rays. Well, in one sense, we will have to do that if we really want to find out how the system responds, because our models aren't good enough. But we take a hell of a chance with the future by doing things like that.

A: You talk a lot about pragmatism and experiential learning (a popular phrase in business schools today). American psychologist and philosopher William James held that the value of any truth was utterly dependent upon its use to the person who held it. He talks about radical empiricism and that the world can never be halted for an entirely objective analysis because, if nothing else, the mind of the observer and the simple act of observation will affect the outcome of any empirical approach to truth since the mind and its experiences are inseparable. That changed how I thought about what you are saying. It's not what we "know" but what we "believe." That is a tremendously important part of how we act in the world around us. Judgments based on experience are just as important as models based on data. And yet, if I can prove something with the probabilities of three significant figures, then I have much more legitimacy to make my claims than to simply say, "I believe the world works that way."

J: Legitimacy is a big issue here. Since the Enlightenment, we have privileged scientific facts. We give them more legitimacy as a belief system on which we act. But when you get to complex systems and you're trying to describe the behavior of the world, this is no longer the case. The kind of rules that are analytically pure, timeless, or general are not adequate to describe these systems. So it becomes a matter of understanding in a pragmatic way, not knowing in the epistemological sense that science provides.

Pragmatism is very important to my arguments about getting to sustainability. But it is unfamiliar to many and widely misunderstood. It does not mean, as those who misquote William James might say, that anything that works is okay. If the end being sought is improper or immoral, pragmatic thinking and acting cannot make the outcome right. Pragmatism is a way of learning from past experience and also from the experience of present actions. Finding the pragmatic truth relies on a continuous inquiry or experiment by a community of learners that ends only when the "theory" developed to explain the latest results successfully explains what is happening and, then and only then, is deemed to be "true." But such truths are always contingent on and subject to being overruled by future experience. Scientific truths are also obtained by such a continuous inquiry, are verified by the scientific community through the peer review process, and are discarded when new results upset the applecart. Because the scientific method is rigorous and tightly bounded, and because the focus of most science is on isolated, small subjects, scientific facts are generally long-lived and appear to be eternal and unchanging. But they are always contingent and falsifiable.

A: Can we bring this down to Earth? I am having a hard time seeing how pragmatism can be applied so readily to some environmental problems, like climate change or persistent chemicals.

J: The ultimate banning of ozone-depleting chemicals fits the pragmatic model. When introduced, these chemicals were truly wonderful and were put to widespread use. But when scientists discovered and agreed that there were serious impacts coming from their use, the truth shifted from wonder to dismay, and the world acted on this new truth and banned their use. Not so for climate change. In spite of the agreement of almost all scientists studying climate change that humans are responsible for the recent acceleration of impacts, nothing consequential is being done. Given the size and dynamics of the global system, the scientific method cannot be rigorously applied. Those who oppose action use this limitation of pure science, to base their arguments on the premise that only "sound science" can serve to ground whatever actions are to be taken. A pragmatist could accept the facts coming from the climate change community, and argue that there is enough known to move ahead, but warily.

It's not only big, complex problems like global warming that would benefit from pragmatic thinking. I recently read that the National Football League Players Association is supporting millions of dollars of research on the effects of repetitive brain trauma in athletes. Now, do we really need to spend millions of dollars to know that running head first into a brick wall is not a healthy thing to do? The call for more scientific data is simply a delaying tactic. Similarly, environmental critic Paul Hawken reminded us in his 1993 book *The Ecology of Commerce* that the earth is finite and that we can't keep draining its resources at a rate that exceeds the rate in which they are replenished. Anyone who has balanced a checkbook knows this pragmatically through experience. Pragmatic thinking often goes by the more familiar name of common sense. While scientific inquiry is important for progress, we must balance it with pragmatic thinking when experience calls for action now. Pragmatists understand that their "solutions" are contingent and may or may not work, but offer the best chance for positive change. They also know that, because they are contingent, they must continue their inquiry and adjust the "solutions" as they produce new answers to their questions.

As business and government have become increasingly technocratic, employing theories from the social sciences, the frame for thinking and acting has become ossified, with two serious consequences. First, the unreality of the theories and models is ignored, resulting in the appearance of serious unintended consequences. Second, the contingency of the solutions being offered is also ignored; attention to the problem quickly wanes on the assumption that "they" got it right the first time. But the world has always changed by the time any solutions are implemented. The machinery necessary to continue the inquiry is rarely included in the resulting programs and budgets. When experience announces to the world that the original problems persist or create others, the whole process must start at square one, without the benefit of the pragmatic learning that might have been acquired. As I have often said, this ossified way of thinking is a primary cause of unsustainability. Pragmatic thinking and acting could and would, in my opinion, open up the possibility of flourishing, and put us on a path toward sustainability. But we would have to kick the habit of framing everything through the lens of objective reality and the scientific method.

A: To me, the upshot of what you're describing is that we can't scientifically theorize sustainability. We can't theorize about the whole world system around us. We have to get involved, engage, and get our hands dirty. We have to experience nature in order to understand and care for it. We can't just live in a totally man-made environment and read about it and theorize it. We have to become part of it. I was trying to think of a practical example to describe what we're talking about and I came up with this. I have an antique car. I'm not a mechanic but I have a mechanic that lets me work with him. I can know in my head how to change the leaf springs or the fuel pump, but getting under the hood and actually doing it is a very different matter. Watching my mechanic work, he has a totally different model for looking at that car, one based on his past experiences and his really knowing a car, not just the repair manual. He can feel it, see it, experience it, and engage it.

J: Andy, absolutely. I often use gardening as the metaphor for mucking around in complexity. Further, I can capture everything you just said in one word, and that word is *possibility*. I use that to define sustainability. It's a possibility. It comes out of our wise and prudent understanding of the world. It means we truly have to live out of an understanding that we are only a part of that interconnected world.

Only someone who has experienced the operation of a complex system can truly understand it. Pragmatism is a philosophical exercise that gets its worldly power through practice, hence its name that is derived from the Greek word for action. As I've said, Humberto Maturana has built a whole theory of human cognition and consciousness on a pragmatic foundation: "learning is doing, doing is learning." We develop our cognitive system on the fly. The beliefs we embody that later underpin what we do come from our earlier experiences. Our "truths" are all pragmatically grounded.

A: You state that "the reality we live depends on the explanatory path we adopt and this, in turn, depends on the emotional domain from which we act." It seems to me that what you're describing is consistent with psychologist Karl Weick's work in which he says, "we enact the world we live in." That's where pragmatism really hit its stride. The world you look at physically may be the same world I look at, but we may see very different worlds. We each bring something to the equation of understanding what's around us. Am I interpreting your ideas correctly?

J: Yes, Andy. That's a very good statement. People construct their worlds out of their being-in-the-world. By being-in-the-world, our bodies and our brains—our cognitive system—grow and develop as we experience life. In an explanatory system of objective reality, there can be only one true answer about everything, and we engage in a contest of domination to determine what that "truth" is. One of us has to win that argument. That is why we still fight wars or say we hate people and things. But in a world of pragmatic thinking, my understanding of the same world that both of us inhabit is likely to be different from yours because you and I have led historically different lives. This realization is important as a fundamental context of love and acceptance, because, as long as people are acting and thinking authentically, no one can own an absolutely "true" belief about the world or claim to have the one "right" way to act.

Think about our shared experiences as student and teacher. I learned with the students. They learned with me. I was their "teacher" because that was the role that I was playing, the identity I was enacting. But that didn't necessarily mean that I always knew more than they did: it didn't necessarily mean that I was smarter. It meant only that I probably had more experience. I was there to bring my experience and capabilities into the room. But to make it really work, I had to love the students. I saw them as human beings, not just students. I cared for them. Reflecting on my years as a teacher, becoming aware of my special relationships with the students was a very important step along the way to finding sustainability, flourishing, and the model of being that so critically informs my work.

A: How can we sum this up in a more practical way? How can companies incorporate pragmatic thinking into their sustainability strategies and structures?

J: I spoke a little about this earlier when I talked about corporate pro-activity by involving stakeholders in decision making to avoid negative consumer activism. Stakeholder involvement is a big topic these days, but few, if any, see its connection to pragmatism. Pragmatic beliefs on which to act (truths) arise during a continuous inquiry by the community of the concerned. That's just another phrase for the stakeholders. I think many business leaders have a badly mistaken idea that being pragmatic is doing whatever works for them as the holder of all that is important to a company. But that is not true; an entire community of interests is essential to any inquiry that is likely to produce useful results. Neighbors would join an inquiry of local issues. Scientists would be invited into conversations about the safety of products or operations. I hear much talk about transparency, but see little happening. Publishing weighty tomes reporting on sustainability performance or CSR activities is not the same as examining the data jointly before and after it gets converted into numbers.

In a more specific context, companies can practice some form of lean manufacturing or other discipline based on continuous improvement. All the popular systems, the Toyota Production System perhaps being the most familiar, are forms of pragmatism. They all rely on a community of learners. Solutions arise from the experience of that community, not from computer and engineering analyses. Pragmatic practices complement the output of technologists who originate new products and services. But as I have said, for all but the simplest cases, their designs are based on incomplete models and will generally lead to unintended consequences and disappointing performance when developed strictly on scientific analysis. Parallel pragmatic processes can often spot issues before they happen and direct the technologists toward effective adaptations.

Echoing much criticism about the shortsighted horizons that corporations use to drive corporate planning and operations, pragmatic practices take patience and continuing commitment to bring a firm's (or any institution's) aspirations into synchrony with the actual outputs, intended and unintended. The centrality of finance to our society has created a mystique about the magical powers of corporate managers that has turned into hubris and produces tin-eared and tunnel-visioned executives, exactly the opposite qualities needed to be pragmatic. I can't count the number of tales about business failures due to arrogance in the executive suite. Here, all it would take is an attitudinal change, but that would be just as hard as talking a junkie out of taking the next dose. But it needs to happen, and not only in the front office. The geniuses in the lab have to become pragmatic about their latest wonderful invention. Remember CFCs or look at the latest flap about the problems using Bisphenol A or the drug Avandia. What looks wonderful in a lab or product development department may act differently in the real world. Again, continuing pragmatic inquiries can lessen the likelihood of creating results that are antagonistic to flourishing.

PART III

LOOKING TO THE FUTURE

CHAPTER 8

Reasons to Be Hopeful

People often ask me if I am optimistic or pessimistic about the future. This is really the wrong question. The right question is, "Am I hopeful?" The answer is an absolute yes! Playwright and first president of the Czech Republic Vaclav Havel said, "Hope is definitely not the same thing as optimism. It is not the conviction that something will turn out well, but the certainty that something makes sense, regardless of how it turns out." It is easy to identify positive (I believe the right) ways to begin to proceed toward sustainability, as my work and that of others already have pointed out. The first step is to isolate the root causes that are driving us in the wrong direction.

As we begin to uncover the root causes of unsustainability, we encounter the way that Cartesian thinking, by its very nature, separates us from the world and distances ourselves from what's real. As we begin to understand and acknowledge this disconnect, we begin to address how to get ourselves out of the present unsustainable state. But it won't happen with more efficient products; rather it will happen with a change of beliefs to reorder our conceptions of who we are and how we connect with the environment.

One component of this reordering, complexity, is slowly being welcomed in the world of science. Though it is not a particularly warm welcome, it is yielding some interesting results. We are developing an appreciation for complexity and the limits of objectivity. There's more recognition that we can't describe the world in its entirety, even with supercomputer models. A second component of this reordering attends to the reasons and motivations for consumption—not just consumptive behavior, but the values of what's behind it. And research has begun on that as well. We are discovering the limits of the standard model of what it is to be human. We're beginning to understand that we are not just bundles of needs with a set of mystical utilities and computers in our heads.

So I'm hopeful in the sense that we are making headway into an understanding of both where we are and where to go. It's a very different approach than is taken in typical greening frameworks for business management and public policy analysis. If we change the reductionist opening to objective reality as the basis for creating the world in which we act, we are also telling the world of education, places such as MIT, Harvard, and Michigan, that "You're doing it wrong." While that's a tough perspective to sell, there are changes that are taking place in these institutions as well. Interdisciplinarity is on the rise. The dominance of narrow disciplines to explain and address the critical problems facing our world seems to be lessening.

As we accept all the components of a new model and lay them side by side with our four-hundred-year-old model of Western modern culture, we are beginning to engage the real sustainability battle. We are recognizing that the dominant culture is itself part of the problem. And with that, we are recalling that there are other fundamental ways to understand what it is to be human. We are starting to live with a new story.

But to realize this shift in thinking more widely, I believe it must manifest itself in the market, where consumers—a relatively untapped source of power for change—begin to take personal responsibility for the way that they live and the way that they consume. For this to happen, the basic model of economic behavior must shift from the present, primary model that is based on a rational machine that decides which transaction to engage according to some preference order or utility. As this flawed story goes, the more information we possess, the more rational will be our decisions to purchase this or that. So one proposed solution to reduce the damaging externalities of the goods sold in the market is to use labeling and scoring systems to shift consuming behavior, but there is increasing evidence that this strategy has little effect. Changes brought about by creating a better-informed and educated consumer will move things in the direction of sustainability, but only slowly and at the margins.

Actions in the marketplace, like all others, are driven primarily by habit and cultural coercion, not by some rational computation. The machinery of the current consumption-driven economy has been fine-tuned to embed the particular habits that serve major producers. Consumer sovereignty, if it ever did exist, is moribund if not dead. The now addictive consumption habits that drive the U.S. economy have to be treated by much more than access to good information. Unfortunately, habits, or more accurately, addictions, are extremely hard to change. Some sort of intervention is usually required. Acknowledgment of one's addiction and appreciation of the harm it is causing are essential first steps to recovery. Occupy Wall Street was spawned in part by Adbusters, a Canadian NGO with a mission to reduce consumption. Their campaigns have had some success, perhaps from their cleverness, but there is little evidence of major and continuing change. The weight of corporations and financial institutions that protect and increase the size of the economy (and their piece of it) overwhelms current efforts to wake up consumers and cure their addiction.

To change how we consume, we must return relationship to the marketplace. The incessant drive toward the impersonality of bigger scale and scope, on the grounds of improved efficiency, has turned the market into a completely lifeless, commoditized institution. Efficiency is arguably good in producing wealth, but not without understanding that it has limits and a negative side. The loss of local economic actors, both producers and merchants, has contributed to the frittering away of community cohesion. The loss of a relationship between employer and employee or between purchaser and seller has converted such engagements to be entirely transactional in nature. There is no human Being in those exchanges anymore. All are economic actors in a market system. The fabled baker of Adam Smith's vision of capitalism, one that served the needs of customers by satisfying his own needs, is gone. In his place is the cold conglomerate with no concern for (or even connection to) the needs of the real, individual customer, just his or her willingness to pay. This loss of relationships is an immense barrier to achieving sustainability, one that has reached a point at which the benefits of more efficient means are more than offset by the deleterious impact on the human beings involved.

What will make this system change? Sustainability advocate and former Greenpeace CEO Paul Gilding believes that some major crisis must come before any significant policy changes will be made. He sees this as a "necessary" step in coming to grips with the reality of both natural and human limits, and is hopeful (there's that word again) that human innovative capability will be able to contend with the challenges we will then face. While I don't disagree with Gilding's prognosis, I hold out hope for another, gentler way. Although we don't know what this portends for the future, we can see glimpses in the way that some forward-thinking corporations are helping their stakeholders care for the world, instead of simply satisfying their needs.

I am intrigued by a recent "innovation" from Patagonia, the outdoor clothing company; one that, important to note, serves a young and affluent market segment. Patagonia ran an ad on Black Friday 2011 with the headline "Don't Buy This Jacket." It was not a spoof but, rather, a reaction to the consumerist frenzy on the Highest Holy Day of our consumerist religion. The ad started with this message:

"It's Black Friday, the day in the year retail turns from red to black and starts to make real money. But Black Friday, and the culture of consumption it reflects, puts the economy of natural systems that support all life firmly in the red. We're now using the resources of one-and-a-half planets on our one and only planet. Because Patagonia wants to be in business for a good long time—and leave a world inhabitable for our kids—we want to do the opposite of every other business today. We ask you to buy less and to reflect before you spend a dime on this jacket or anything else."

The ad ended with

> "There is much to be done and plenty for us all to do. Don't buy
> what you don't need. Think twice before you buy anything. Go to
> patagonia.com/CommonThreads or scan the QR code below. Take
> the Common Threads Initiative pledge, and join us in the fifth 'R,'
> to reimagine a world where we take only what nature can replace."

Common Threads is an exchange set up by Patagonia to encourage
people to buy used Patagonia stuff on eBay before going to the store to
buy it new. This represents a new story, a new way of thinking, one that
has business school professors scratching their heads and looking for
some market-based, utilitarian rationality to explain. But Patagonia has
been a leader in greening businesses since that idea began, and this kind
of innovative thinking is more about being authentic to their values
than trying to capture more market share. I read a story about this ad in
the blog *GreenBiz.com* that exemplifies the need by some experts to explain all corporate rationality as leading to increased sales. The reporter
raised a question about the wisdom of their action.

> "That's good environmental messaging. But is it good business for a
> company to urge people to buy less? Moreover, is there a disconnect
> between this ad and Patagonia's own plans to grow, open new stores
> and mail out more catalogs?"

This reporter may be forcing the paradigm of the old story on a new
phenomenon that it is ill-prepared to explain. This advance is consistent
with who Patagonia is, a company whose first green move some years
ago was to set a limit on growth, close some stores, and cut the number
of items in their catalog. They were an early user of lifecycle assessment
to understand the impacts of their products. They were a pioneer in the
use of organic cotton. The ad they ran has environmental impact information for the jacket they are telling us not to buy. Patagonia has a huge
advantage over most companies in going green. It has a loyal consumer
base and a high price point. It is privately held, mostly, if not entirely,

by its founder, Yvon Chouinard. It can do whatever Chouinard wants without worrying about the impact on its stock price. As a professional mountaineer, he was concerned about the environment even before he founded the company.

To me, what the company is doing is changing its story toward one of sustainability-as-flourishing. It represents a challenge to the dominant model while also exposing the resistance to that challenge from within the model itself. The ad says, don't buy this unless you "need" it and have thought carefully about its environmental implications. While more indirectly stated than the question about the environment, the ad is asking people to reflect on the idea of need. If they didn't want anybody to buy it, Patagonia would have simply withdrawn it from their line of jackets. Patagonia is still a business that must sell its goods to survive, but they are quite clear about how they want to earn the right to operate. I continue to admire their stance and commitments, and recognize the challenges they face in going against the tide. Messages like the one they sent out can contribute to the dimming of consumerism, a good idea for humans and the environment, and return consumption to a process that is consciously and wisely practiced.

And it is not just small private companies that are starting to push the boundaries of the dominant model. There are also large manufacturing firms, such as Interface, Inc. The late company founder Ray Anderson used to talk about climbing Mount Sustainability to explain that the company couldn't keep doing what they had been doing. He literally woke up one morning with the realization that he had to rebuild the company from the bottom up. Doing that was not easy and produced a bunch of hard knocks. His strategies didn't always work, but Anderson kept pushing the issue down to the people on the floor, encouraging them to think about who they were, to realize the systemic characteristic of the world and the unintended consequences of business as usual. He was one of the very first corporate leaders to accept that the company is part of the complex web of life. He hired every big sustainability name in the world—including Amory Lovins, Bill McDonough, and Paul Hawken—and created his Dream Team. His efforts paid off, and Interface today is still a company that has the ideas, not all the ideas I would like to see them have, but most of the ideas that are very critical to slowing down and eventually reversing this juggernaut that is pushing us toward collapse. It's a good start, but there is so much farther to go to realize the positive vision of sustainability.

"I hold out hope for the future. The culture is changing, albeit slowly, to acting through and living by a new story."

Given these few examples and the cultural challenge they present, I hold out hope for the future. The culture is changing, albeit slowly, to acting through and living by a new story. In fact, I believe we are on the threshold of a new opportunity to recover our consciousness of the interconnected nature of the world and our place within (not outside of) it. The increasing attention to complexity keeps a fire burning under our intellectual kettles. Natural and man-made catastrophes remind us that there is much we don't know that we don't know. But as the social and natural worlds change, as they have been for years, the old tools and rules will be seen more and more as part of the problem, not the solution. New ones are essential. We can see parts of society that are adopting them, notably young people who reject the broken social and natural worlds as bestowed to them and reject the purely Cartesian worldview. They are the first to enter the authentic mode of living in which every individual takes responsibility for the full consequences of their actions. They are taking a conscious commitment to stop following the crowd. They are my glimpse into a future world of hope.

Andy: In this final chapter of the book you say that you are hopeful but you make a careful point to say that hope is different from optimism. Why is *hopeful* a better word?

John: Optimism springs from some confidence based on a technical assessment that you're doing things that have worked in the past and therefore you can rationally say, "This is going to work." That's not where we are. All the evidence says that the way we are running and understanding the world isn't working. So I am not optimistic in that strict sense. But I am hopeful. Hope is different. Hope is really a belief in the rightness of what you're doing. In Vaclav Havel's words, it is "the certainty that something makes sense." American social critic Christopher Lasch adds, "Hope implies a deep-seated trust in life that appears absurd to those who lack it. . . . Improvidence, a blind faith that things will somehow work out for the best, furnishes a poor substitute for the disposition to see things through even when they don't." In fact, American poet William Stanley Merwin even goes so far as to say that you can be both hopeful and pessimistic at the same time, adding, "You make a decision to be hopeful. When you're in a lifeboat, that's not the time for your worst behavior, but for your best."

I'm quite hopeful that the ideas and concepts that others and I are talking about with respect to sustainability are the right ones to move us away from where we are. The power of this notion of hope has been demonstrated over human history for centuries. Societies have faced crises; they have lost the ability to run themselves. But right at the very bottom, they have found hope. The people dedicated themselves to solving their problems, regardless of the "rational" data-driven reasons to give up. They wrote entirely new stories to guide them. That's what hope is all about.

A: Oberlin College environmental studies professor David Orr says, "Optimism is the recognition that the odds are in your favor; hope is the faith that things will work out whatever the odds. Hope is a verb with its sleeves rolled up." That notion helps me when people ask me if I am discouraged. It's saying, "When I get discouraged, we still have to try." Do you personally get discouraged?

J: Of course I get discouraged from time to time. It's impossible not to, but mostly I am impatient, as I said. I see people behaving in a way I don't think is particularly sensible. They are deeply mired in the old ways. They're not moving or trying new ways. They don't accept that the old ways have stopped producing what they're looking for. But I'm one person in a big world. It's hard to get discouraged when I'm spending most of the remaining part of my life thinking about the future. I have a vision; I think it's a good vision. I don't expect to get there in my lifetime, but that's not a matter to be discouraged about.

A: In an interview in *Smithsonian* magazine, Dennis Meadows, co-author of *Limits to Growth*, said that he no longer believes that sustainable development is feasible. He said, "When I use the term sustainable development—which I consider to be an oxymoron actually—I am trying to capture the meaning that most people seem to have. In so far as I can tell, people who use the term mean, essentially, that this would be a phase of development where they get to keep what they have but all the poor people can catch up. Or, they get to keep doing what they've been doing, but through the magic of technology they are going to cause less damage to the environment and use fewer resources. Either way you use the term, it is just a fantasy. Neither of those is possible—anymore. It probably was possible back in the 1970s, but not now. We're at 150 percent of the global carrying capacity." I read that and it makes me feel discouraged. I keep pushing because it's better than just giving up. But it sometimes feels like the task before us is insurmountable.

J: I completely agree with Dennis Meadows, but he's talking about sustainable development. I'm not. I'm talking about a notion of sustainability that's radically different. Like Dennis, I do not believe that it's possible to do what the Brundtland Commission proposed; the idea that we can continue to base our political economy on growth and efficiency. That's not what sustainability is all about for me. Sustainability-as-flourishing does not depend on a technical solution or some kind of magic efficiency, the kind that Dennis is talking about. That just isn't going to happen. Sustainability, as I talk about it, rests on a shift in our consciousness about who we are and a consequent realization that wealth is not the be-all and end-all. What matters is who we are as human beings. We don't need all the trappings of modernity to recover our humanness. A shift in our fundamental way of thinking about the world; how we govern, respect, and become a part of it is distinctly possible, as is any mind-set shift. I am hopeful that we can make it, and continue to enjoy life on this planet.

A: I'd like to hear more about your hope and what you see with the lens you have on. Can you give us a little sense of what you've seen change over the course of your extensive work and thinking in this area?

J: I have seen a global consciousness arise out of a sharpened awareness of the criticality of the Earth system to human and other life. This new consciousness can be traced back to the 1960s, and without it, there would be little understanding of the situation we're in now. We would not have institutions in place to take care of these concerns. I see new forms of institutions springing up based on Care, rather than some materialistic purpose. The Arab Spring demonstrates the power of solidarity—publicly caring for others. While the Rio+20 conference was disappointing, with virtually nothing moving at the global governance level, thousands of NGO members joined to create programs outside the machinery of government. I see the business sector getting serious about lightening our environmental load, and that gives me hope. The same goes for schools of business or management, but I do wish both would learn to use the right language when they talk about what they are doing. While I am often a critic of the new social media technologies, I do see their potential in facilitating the growth of local social movements into national or global forces. Small-scale social experiments exploring local economies or co-housing and other kinds of material goods are proving that other forms of capitalism can work. Unfortunately, I don't see those in power paying much attention.

A: I often tell my students that we're in the midst of an "energy renaissance." We can put different things in our vehicles to make them go, we can buy energy from an expanding array of sources, and we can talk about lighting and appliance efficiency in common language. Every major maker of automobiles offers a hybrid, and a few have an all-electric vehicle for sale. The changes are not just technical. They are cultural too. People are thinking about energy and their energy footprint (or cost) in a more serious way. To me, that's a change in consciousness. But the funny thing about a renaissance is that most people don't know we're in one until it's over. We feel the pain as we discussed earlier; the anger over the idea of the end of what we knew, and the thought of having to trade our incandescent light bulbs for compact fluorescent light bulbs (CFLs), for example. But the world is changing nonetheless.

J: I'm a little leery about using consciousness when we talk about a collective entity. For me, only individual humans can be conscious. I think we use this phrase to explain our observations that a lot of people have become conscious of the same new things. They have adopted new ideas and belief structures that have, in turn, created emerging social norms. But even with that, I am skeptical that we are really in the midst of an energy renaissance. Almost all of the talk of responding to climate change and to the possibility that fossil fuels will run out is focused on technological fixes.

I wonder how many people would buy CFLs if they weren't often highly subsidized by energy companies; if we really had to pay the full price for them. The first big purchase of CFLs I made was at a sale where one of the local power companies was effectively giving them away. For ten bucks I probably bought a hundred and fifty dollars' worth of CFLs. That was only about a year ago. I don't think there's much change of consciousness, certainly not in the United States. I think our values and beliefs are, if anything, becoming more entrenched in the mainstream.

A: Do you see glimpses around the periphery? We have local food production and community-supported agriculture (CSAs); the LOHAS consumers (Lifestyle of Health and Sustainability) that amounted to more than $300 billion in sales in 2007. John Wellinghoff, chair of the Federal

Energy Regulatory Commission, issued a controversial ruling in 2012 that utilities will soon have to pay big customers full market rate for the power they save during peak periods. Certainly these are signs of change?

J: Yes, there are certainly glimmerings. Some people are living off the grid. There's an incipient movement of transition towns; communities that are accepting that fossil fuels are going to run out and are changing their local norms and institutions in anticipation. The United Kingdom has taken the lead on a variety of programs to relocalize the economy. In western Massachusetts, not far from Lexington, where I live, a number of neighboring towns are using their own currency, Berkshares, for locally sourced goods and services. Time banking, an alternative monetary system that uses time instead of money as a form of reciprocal service exchange, is strong in England and northern Europe. People are building an economy within an economy. It's still capitalism, still uses money in most cases, but uses barter or time banking in others, and focuses on reintroducing local relationships to market activities. This complements the primary economy and begins to rebuild connections and community, both of which are absolutely critical to the idea of flourishing. We cannot flourish as isolated individuals: we only can flourish through our connectedness to the world.

Some recent political events also indicate a shift in consciousness, and also provide evidence of emerging solidarity. Occupy Wall Street is one of the very few examples in the United States in which people have stood up for solidarity. "We are the 99 percent." The solidarity shown by that movement was very important, even in the absence of closely associated changes. The growing acceptance of gay marriage is a major change in the winds of social norms that goes beyond deeply embedded social traditions. It recognizes the real meaning of love, the kind of love I have discussed as the acceptance of all human beings as they are, rather than as defined by some institutional definition. That polls show more than half the people in this country accepting gay unions could very well be a precursor and an opening to shifting social norms. This would be a huge stride toward making flourishing possible.

A: Do you see social change in business? I am very excited by the emergence of the hybrid or B Corporation. These new corporate organizations legally operate in the blurry space between the for-profit and nonprofit worlds and introduce a whole different set of values to the business sector. They challenge the deeply embedded notion that the "social responsibility of business is to increase its profits," as economist Milton Friedman so famously said.

J: I think you're right on. The idea of the B Corporation that exists for producing social and environmental benefits is a significant move. How this innovation takes hold is a story that's still being written. But these glimmerings contribute to my hopefulness. These and other similar changes are the "right things to do." We're far from knowing how they're going to turn out. It's much too soon. But they do create possibility. There's more. Cooperatives and employee-owned companies are alternative forms of businesses that share ownership with customers and workers. They are part of a growing movement, particularly in Europe, that says corporations are not just about shareholders. These all are hopeful signs. They're emerging at this time because people don't accept the status quo anymore. Many younger entrepreneurially minded graduates and a lot of just plain folks want to start and work for companies whose values are about caring for the world.

A: In other parts of our conversation, you have been very critical of consumption, and then in this section you say that the consumer is a source of untapped power for creating sustainability-as-flourishing. How do you explain this juxtaposition?

J: Consumers can exert a great deal of influence over corporations, just like voters can exert a great deal of influence over the political structure. So as consumers start turning away from products that are being purchased to feed some addiction and can't satisfy them, and seek goods to help them authentically care for themselves and others in the world, then they become able to push back very hard on corporations. Signs of this are happening. Today's young people have access to all the new social media and technology that can quickly generate very large responses. My generation, even if we wanted to boycott Walmart, would have had a hard time simply because such mass communication was difficult. But today a boycott against Walmart or any other company can happen overnight; go viral. These new tools also give me hope.

A: Through this entire conversation, we have been talking about change in different domains. While I think that business is important (otherwise I wouldn't be teaching at a business school), I also think that religion and education are critically important. They are the only institutions that can speak to our values directly. When people hear about sustainability or climate change from a church, mosque, synagogue, or temple, they will internalize it in a far more powerful way than any price signal can create. And when they take classes in K–12 or the university that give them lessons on how to think about the world in a sustainable way, I think that is a tremendous sign of hope.

J: It's interesting that you mention these two institutions. I have been involved for a year with a group at the Weatherhead Business School at Case Western Reserve on a project thinking about the role of spirituality in business and business schools. I was surprised to be asked to work on this topic, but I jumped at it because, as you mention, this is a real opening for sustainability.

I'm particularly interested in spirituality, but not limited to religious settings. Organized religions are the right place for inspiration but not change. Their images, concepts, and values are thousands of years old in some cases, and they haven't caught up with the modern world and the pervasiveness of unsustainability. They have a hard time getting beyond good and evil, but the problems we are talking about are more about how to live in a finite, complex world. Spirituality is a different notion. Among other qualities, it always raises consciousness of interconnectedness. This is consistent with an idea my colleagues at Case Western have offered, that spirituality is connected to a kind of immanence, force, or universal consciousness in the world. David Bohm, the physicist, talks about quantum mechanics as having some inexplicable aspects that are attributed to some kind of (so far) undetectable universal field. I don't have to believe this particular explanation (and remain agnostic) to appreciate how important spirituality, or the web of life, is to sustainability. I think it is remarkable that this interest in spirituality is showing up in a business school, hardly a place where conversation strays far from talk about competition and market share. I have taught a module on examining sustainability through a spiritual lens at the Marlboro Graduate School, but this is far from introducing this idea at a mainline business school like Weatherhead.

A: I find it interesting that you have been teaching at—if you don't mind my saying—an alternative school, whereas you formerly taught at a mainstream school, MIT. You've seen it from both sides. Do you see these changes coming from the fringe or from the mainstream of the business school world?

J: It's coming from both, but the fringes are more open to these ideas than the mainstream. There are only three or four of the sort of schools that you call "alternative." The ones I know are Marlboro in Brattleboro, Vermont; Bainbridge, outside of Seattle; and Presidio in San Francisco. These particular schools are all located in the shadow of the counterculture of the 1960s and 1970s, when people were more open to radical thinking. Sustainability-as-flourishing is radical; it's a disruptive idea, as Harvard Business School professor Clay Christensen might say. It forces confrontation with change, and change is hard at all schools, especially at elite schools. The culture in universities is very conservative and chopped up into many disparate disciplines. Disciplines come and go on the basis of their central ideas and premises; disciplinarians don't want to go away so they tenaciously hold on to their premises. But many of the people teaching at places such as Marlboro and Bainbridge are untenured, adjunct faculty who are not married to a discipline. So the context is different. The fringe is simply more open to radical ideas.

A: Let's bring this conversation and this book to a close by focusing on where the most hope lies. To me, that's with young people. When people ask me if I am hopeful, and I say yes, they often say, "That's because you're around young people." I say, "Absolutely." I see in young people today a greater desire to think about their lives in terms of a vocation or a purpose. They want to dedicate themselves toward making the world a better place, to make it more sustainable, to flourishing. It's not all, nor even the majority, but a significant number, and that's all that's necessary to make change possible. That's what gives me hope.

J: Without question, Andy, I agree. What we are talking about here is a cultural transformation, a paradigmatic change that is going to take generations to become firmly rooted.

My generation is done for. We're old and we've done our thing. Most of my former colleagues are retired and holding on. It's today's young that are going to grow into positions of leadership and power. They are the ones that are going to make things happen. But I don't think that even the young adults of today are going to be the ones to ultimately change things. They are part of a much longer process of change that will even outlive them. It will take generations for these ideas to become embedded in the culture and new norms aligned with flourishing to arise. I can't see anything like this happening in my lifetime or perhaps even in the lifetimes of my grandchildren. We are most likely stuck with today's basic political economy unless it completely falls apart under the stress of inequality, commodification, and global collapse.

A: What advice do you have for young people who care about sustainability-as-flourishing? How should they think about their careers and their lives?

J: The one area in which we have more control than anything else is our own idea about who we are and how the world works. It's going to be very hard to change the character of the workplace and polling place. And while it is important to try to change these things, the fact is that a solidly entrenched set of institutions and powerful people is not going to go away without a struggle.

But even in the face of such opposition, every aware individual can change his or her own worldview and values. I have already outlined what I believe are the right beliefs for sustainability-as-flourishing. Everyone must ask himself or herself, "What gives you the authentic and most lasting sense of well-being and fullness in your life?" I'm convinced that when young people ask themselves that question, they will always come down to how they care for people, and how they care for the world. So my advice would be to start there; truly start there. If you need help, go get it. There are plenty of coaches that have the same view of what it is to be human that I talk about. But take the first step yourself and dedicate yourselves to living an authentic life.

A: John, thank you very much. I have really enjoyed this conversation. It's a little like being back in the classroom with you, although I am a slightly older student than when I was last there. But I really enjoyed returning and learning from you through these discussions.

J: Andy, I am more than slightly older. I have learned from our conversation as well. Thinking is not a static or solitary activity. It doesn't happen in my head or in your head. It happens in our conversations. So I appreciate your willingness to hang in there through these conversations with me. We let ourselves ramble a bit and hopefully—there's that word again—our ramblings will produce something that's useful and can make a difference; turn people on and get them to think critically. But in the end, it is up to the young people to come up with the kind of changes that are absolutely essential to transform the world to one of flourishing.

As we have been talking, I have been thinking about the idea of a story, trying to remember a good one to exemplify the skeleton holding together all the ideas we have covered. Techies like me are not very good storytellers, so I turn to the more literate world. I recently watched a children's dramatic adaptation of Antoine de Saint-Exupéry's *The Little Prince* and reread the original story shortly afterward. The whole story is built around the themes that I have been talking about with you: Caring, pragmatism, and the dangers of narrow-mindedness (ideological thinking) among others. The fox that meets the Little Prince in the desert delivers these themes allegorically. "[Taming] is an act too often neglected, said the fox. It means to establish ties. . . . You become responsible, forever, for what you have tamed." It would be very hard to find more evocative words to describe Caring. But perhaps the line that touches me the most is the secret the fox tells to the Prince as he says goodbye. "It is only with the heart that one can see rightly; what is essential is invisible to the eye." This is a great metaphor for Care. Someday, when flourishing comes home, the poets among us will write the story, but until then, each one of us will have to work with the ideas without the fabric a better storyteller can weave.

Recommended Readings
and Bibliography

Contemporary Critiques

Berry, W. *The Unsettling of America: Culture and Agriculture*. San Francisco: Sierra Club, 1996.

Diamond, J. *Collapse: How Societies Choose to Fail of Succeed*. New York: Viking Penguin, 2004.

Ehrlich, P. *The Population Bomb*. San Francisco: Sierra Club, 1969.

Friedman, T. *Hot, Flat, and Crowded: Why We Need a Green Revolution—and How It Can Renew America*. New York: Farrar, Straus and Giroux, 2008.

Gilding, P. *The Great Disruption: Why the Climate Crisis Will Bring On the End of Shopping and the Birth of a New World*. New York: Bloomsbury Press, 2011.

Kasser, T. *The High Price of Materialism*. Cambridge, MA: MIT Press, 2002.

Korten, D. *When Corporations Rule the World*. San Francisco: Berrett-Koehler, 1995.

Lasch, C. *The Culture of Narcissism: American Life in an Era of Diminished Expectations*. New York: W. W. Norton, 1978.

McKibben, B. *Deep Economy: The Wealth of Communities and the Durable Future*. New York: Times Books, 2007.

McKibben, B. *Eaarth: Making Life on a Tough New Planet*. New York: St. Martin's Griffin, 2010.

Porritt, J. *Capitalism as If the World Matters*. London: Earthscan, 2007.

Putnam, R. *Bowling Alone: The Collapse and Revival of American Community*. New York: Simon & Schuster, 2000.

Orr, D. *Earth in Mind: On Education, Environment, and the Human Prospect*. Washington DC: Island Press, 1994.

Sandel, M. *What Money Can't Buy: The Moral Limits of Markets*. New York: Farrar, Straus and Giroux, 2012.

Schor, J. *Plenitude*. New York: Penguin Books, 2010.

Speth, J. G. *The Bridge at the Edge of the World: Capitalism, the Environment, and Crossing from Crisis to Sustainability.* New Haven, CT: Yale University Press, 2008.

Wilkinson, R., and K. Pickett. *The Spirit Level: Why Greater Equality Makes Societies Stronger.* New York: Bloomsbury Press, 2010.

Sustainability

Brown, L. *Plan B—Rescuing a Planet Under Stress and a Civilization in Trouble.* New York: W.W. Norton, 2003.

Ehrenfeld, J. *Sustainability by Design: A Subversive Strategy for Transforming Our Consumer Culture.* New Haven, CT: Yale University Press, 2008.

United Nations World Commission on Environment and Development. *Our Common Future.* New York: Oxford University Press, 1987.

Environmental Awareness

Carson, R. *Silent Spring.* Boston: Houghton-Mifflin, 1962.

Fuller, R. B. *Operating Manual for Spaceship Earth.* Carbondale: Southern Illinois University Press, 1969.

Goleman, D., L. Bennett, and Z. Barlow. *Ecoliterate: How Educators Are Cultivating Emotional, Social and Ecological Intelligence.* San Francisco: Jossey-Bass, 2012.

Leopold, A. *A Sand County Almanac and Sketches Here and There.* New York: Oxford University Press, 1949.

McKibben, B. *The End of Nature.* New York: Random House, 1989.

McKibben, B. *Enough: Staying Human in an Engineering Age.* New York: Times Books, 2003.

Merchant, C. *The Death of Nature: Women, Ecology and the Scientific Revolution.* San Francisco: HarperCollins, 1980.

Reisner, M. *Cadillac Desert: The American West and Its Disappearing Water.* New York: Viking, 1986.

Thoreau, H. D. *Walden.* New York: Library of America, 2010.

Social and Organizational Change

Christensen, C. M. *The Innovator's Dilemma: When New Technologies Cause Great Firms to Fail.* Boston: Harvard Business School Press, 1997.

Elkington, J., and P. Hartigan. *The Power of Unreasonable People.* Cambridge, MA: Harvard Business School Press, 2008.

Hawken, P. *Blessed Unrest: How the Largest Movement in the World Came into Being and Why No One Saw It Coming.* New York: Viking, 2007.

Lewin, K. *Resolving Social Conflicts.* New York: Harper & Row, 1948.

Scharmer, C. O. *Theory U: Leading from the Future as It Emerges.* San Francisco: Berrett-Koehler, 2009.

Weick, K. E. *The Social Psychology of Organizing.* Reading, MA: Addison-Wesley, 1969.

Social Sciences

Beck, U. *Risk Society: Toward a New Modernity.* London: Sage, 1992.

Csikszentmihalyi, M. *Flow: The Psychology of Optimal Experience.* New York: HarperPerennial, 2008.

Douglas, M., and B. Isherwood. *The World of Goods.* New York: Basic Books, 1979.

Durkheim, E. *Suicide: A Study in Sociology.* Translated by J. Spaulding & G. Simpson. New York: Free Press, 1951 (1897).

Fromm, E. *To Have or To Be?* New York: Harper & Row, 1976.

Giddens, A. *The Constitution of Society.* Berkeley, CA: University of California Press, 1984.

Golden-Biddle, K., and J. Dutton (eds.). *Using a Positive Lens to Explore Social Change and Organizations.* New York: Routledge, 2012.

Laing, R. D. *Politics of Experience.* New York: Pantheon, 1983.

Maslow, A. H. *Motivation and Personality.* New York: Longman, 1954.

Triandis, H. *Interpersonal Behavior.* Monterey, CA: Brooks-Cole, 1977.

Weber, M. *The Protestant Ethic and The Spirit of Capitalism.* Translated by S. Kalberg. Oxford, UK: Roxbury, 1905 (2002).

Whyte, W. *The Organization Man.* New York: Simon & Schuster, 1956.

Philosophy

Descartes, R. *Discourse on Method.* Upper Saddle River, NJ: Prentice-Hall, 1997.

Evernden, N. *The Natural Alien: Humankind and Environment.* Toronto: Toronto Press, 1985.

Heidegger, M. *Being and Time.* New York: Harper & Row, 1962.

Sessions, G. *Deep Ecology for the 21st Century: Readings on the Philosophy.* Boston: Shambhala, 1995.

James, W. *Writings 1902–1910: The Varieties of Religious Experience / Pragmatism / A Pluralistic Universe / The Meaning of Truth / Some Problems of Philosophy / Essays.* New York: Library of America, 1988.

Kant, I. *Critique of Practical Reason.* Mineola, NY: Dover, 1994.

Kuhn, T. *The Structure of Scientific Revolutions.* Chicago: Chicago University Press, 1962.

Whitehead, A. N. *Science and the Modern World.* New York: Free Press, 1967 (1925).

Economics

Daly, H. *Steady-State Economics.* Washington, DC: Island Press, 1977.

Daly, H. *Beyond Growth: The Economics of Sustainable Development.* Boston: Beacon Press, 1997.

Daly, H., and J. Cobb. *For the Common Good: Redirecting the Economy Toward Community, the Environment and a Sustainable Future.* Boston: Beacon Press, 1994.

Friedman, M. "The Social Responsibility of Business Is to Increase Its Profits." *The New York Times Magazine,* September 13 (1970): 41–67, 71–72.

Heilbroner, R. "Looking Forward: Does Socialism Have a Future?" *The Nation,* 257 (1993): 312.

Heinberg, R. *The End of Growth.* Gabriola Island, BC: New Society, 2011.

Jackson, T. *The Earthscan Reader on Sustainable Consumption.* Sterling, VA: Earthscan, 2000.

Jackson, T. *Prosperity Without Growth: Economics for a Finite Planet.* Oxford, UK: Routledge, 2011.

Marglin, S. *The Dismal Science: How Thinking Like an Economist Undermines Community.* Cambridge, MA: Harvard University Press, 2008.

Max-Neef, M. A. *Human Scale Development: Conception, Application and Further Reflections.* Lanham, MD: Apex, 1989.

Sachs, J. *The End of Poverty: Economic Possibilities for Our Time.* New York: Penguin Press, 2005.

Schumacher, E. F. *Small Is Beautiful: Economics as If People Mattered.* New York: Harper & Row, 1973.

Sen, A. *Development as Freedom.* New York: Oxford University Press, 1999.

Simon, H. *The Sciences of the Artificial,* Second Edition. Cambridge, MA: MIT Press, 1981.

Stiglitz, J. *Globalization and Its Discontents.* New York: W. W. Norton, 2002.

Systems Thinking

Capra, F. *The Web of Life.* New York: Anchor, 1996.

Meadows, D., J. Randers, and D. Meadows. *Beyond the Limits.* Post Mills, VT: Chelsea Green, 1992.

Meadows, D., D. Meadows, J. Randers, and W. Behrens. *The Limits to Growth.* New York: Universe, 1972.

Senge, P. *The Fifth Discipline.* New York: Doubleday/Currency, 1990.

Business and the Environment

Anderson, R. *Mid-Course Correction: Toward a Sustainable Enterprise.* Atlanta: Peregrinzilla Press, 1998.

Bansal, P., and A. Hoffman (eds.). *The Oxford Handbook of Business and the Natural Environment.* Oxford, UK: Oxford University Press, 2012.

Elkington, J. *Cannibals with Forks: The Triple Bottom Line for 21st Century Business.* Oxford: Capstone, 1998.

Esty, D., and A. Winston. *Green to Gold: How Smart Companies Use Environmental Strategy to Innovate, Create Value and Build Competitive Advantage.* New Haven: Yale University Press, 2006.

Hart, S. *Capitalism at the Crossroads: The Unlimited Business Opportunities in Solving the World's Most Difficult Problems.* Upper Saddle River, NJ: Wharton School Publishing, 2005.

Hawken, P. *The Ecology of Commerce.* New York: HarperBusiness, 1993.

Hawken, P., A. Lovins, and H. Lovins. *Natural Capitalism: Creating the Next Industrial Revolution.* New York: Little, Brown, 1999.

Hoffman, A. *From Heresy to Dogma: An Institutional History of Corporate Environmentalism.* Stanford, CA: Stanford Business Books, 2001.

Howard-Grenville, J. *Corporate Culture and Environmental Practice.* Northampton, MA: Edward Elgar, 2007.

Laszlo, C. *Sustainable Value: How the World's Leading Companies Are Doing Well by Doing Good.* Palo Alto, CA: Stanford University Press, 2008.

Lovins, A., H. Lovins, and E. von Weizsacker. *Factor Four.* London: Earthscan, 1998.

McDonough, W., and Braungart, M. *Cradle to Cradle.* New York: North Point Press, 2002.

Schmidheiny, S. *Changing Course: A Global Business Perspective on Development and the Environment.* Cambridge, MA: MIT Press, 1992.

Other

Campbell, J. *The Mythic Image.* Princeton, NJ: Princeton University Press, 1974.

Havel, V. *The Power of the Powerless.* Armonk, NY: M. E. Sharpe, 1985.

Maturana, H. R., and F. J. Varela. *The Tree of Knowledge.* Boston: New Science Library, 1988.

Shepard, H. "On the Realization of Human Potential: Path with a Heart." In David Kolb and others (eds.), *The Organizational Behavior Reader.* Englewood Cliffs, NJ: Prentice-Hall, 1991.

White, L. "The Historical Roots of our Ecological Crisis," *Science, 155*(3767), (1967): 1203–1207.

About the Authors

JOHN R. EHRENFELD retired in 2000 as the director of the MIT Program on Technology, Business, and Environment, an interdisciplinary educational, research, and policy program, having returned in 1985 to MIT, his alma mater, after a long career in the environmental field. He retired again in June 2009 as executive director of the International Society for Industrial Ecology after guiding its development from its founding in 2000. He continues to do research, write, and teach, most recently at several emerging MBA for Sustainability programs. He is an active member of the Harvard Institute for Learning in Retirement and knows that lifelong learning is good for one's health. His honors include the first Lifetime Achievement Award for his academic accomplishments in the field of business and environment, given by the World Resources Institute; the Founders Award for Distinguished Service from the Academy of Management's Organization and Natural Environment Division; and the Society Prize awarded by the International Society for Industrial Ecology. He spent part of the 1998–1999 academic year at the Technical University of Lisbon as a Fulbright Distinguished Scholar and was a visiting professor at the Technical University of Delft during the 2000–2001 academic year. He has served on numerous boards and advisory committees. He is an editor of the *Journal of Industrial Ecology*. He holds B.S. and Sc.D. degrees in chemical engineering from MIT, and is author or coauthor of over two hundred papers, books, reports, and other publications. He spends his summers on the Maine coast and is an avid saltwater fly fisherman.

ANDREW J. HOFFMAN is the Holcim (U.S.) Professor of Sustainable Enterprise at the University of Michigan; a position that holds joint appointments at the Stephen M. Ross School of Business and the School of Natural Resources & Environment. Within this role, Professor Hoffman also serves as director of the Frederick A. and Barbara M. Erb Institute for Global Sustainable Enterprise. Professor Hoffman's research uses a sociological perspective to understand the cultural and institutional aspects of environmental issues for organizations.

He has published over one hundred articles as well as eleven books, which have been translated into five languages. Among his list of honors, he has been awarded the *JMI* Breaking the Frame Award (2012), the Connecticut Book Award (2011), the Aldo Leopold Fellowship (2011), the Aspen Environmental Fellowship (2011 and 2009), the Manos Page Prize (2009), the Faculty Pioneer Award (2003), the Rachel Carson Prize (2001), and the Klegerman Award (1995). His work has been covered in numerous media outlets, including the *New York Times*, *Scientific American*, *Time*, the *Wall Street Journal*, *The Atlantic*, and *National Public Radio*. Prior to academics, Professor Hoffman worked for the U.S. Environmental Protection Agency (Region 1), Metcalf & Eddy Environmental Consultants, T&T Construction & Design, and the Amoco Corporation. He serves on advisory boards of the Michigan League of Conservation Voters, Next Era Energy Trust, SustainAbility, the Earth Portal, the Center for Environmental Innovation, Canopy Partnership, and the *Stanford Social Innovation Review*. Professor Hoffman completed his doctoral degree in 1995 from the Sloan School of Management and the Department of Civil & Environmental Engineering at MIT.

Index

Adbusters, 121
American Dream, 9, 31
Anderson, Ray, 5, 124–25
Arab Spring, 5, 72–73, 128
Arthur Andersen, 4
authenticity, 82–83, 86–87, 92–93, 95
Avandia, 115

B Corporations, 131
Bacon, Francis, 105
Bainbridge Graduate Institute, 90, 133
BAU (business as usual)/BAAU (business almost as usual), 51, 54
Being versus Having, 7, 18, 25–26, 74, 83–84, 88, 89, 91–93, 99, 104, 106
Berkshares, 130
Beyond the Limits (Meadows, Randers, and Meadows, 1992), 90
Bhutan, 76
Bisphenol A, 115
Black Friday, 122
Bohm, David, 132
Bowling Alone (Putnam, 2000), 85
BP oil spill in Gulf of Mexico, 4
Brundtland Commission, 2, 6, 19, 24–25, 29, 50, 127
Buffet, Warren, 72, 94
Bush, George W., 51

business and environment studies, viii
business as usual (BAU)/business almost as usual (BAAU), 51, 54
business education
    corporate sustainability and, 49, 62–63
    Ehrenfeld's influence on, vii–viii
    experiential learning and, 108
    and the future, 123, 128, 132–33
    leadership and, 93
businesses. *See* corporate sustainability

Campbell, Joseph, 91
capitalism. *see* economics
caring, 17, 25, 67, 74, 83–88, 89, 91–92, 105–6, 128, 131, 136
Carnegie Foundation, 72
Carson, Rachel, 106
Carter, Jimmy, ix
Cartesian thinking and René Descartes, 7, 35–36, 46, 89, 101–2, 105, 119, 125
Case Western Reserve, Weatherhead Business School, 132
CFCs (chlorofluorocarbons), 39
CFLs (compact fluorescent light bulbs), 129
China, 68, 70, 71

chlorofluorocarbons (CFCs), 39
Chouinard, Yvon, 124
Christensen, Clay, 133
climate change/global warming, 38,
    60, 71, 110
Coca-Cola, 4, 60
Collapse (Diamond, 2004), 85
Common Threads, 123
community-supported agriculture
    (CSAs), 129
compact fluorescent light bulbs
    (CFLs), 129
complexity of systems, 99–100, 102,
    107–8, 112, 119, 125
concept of sustainability, 15–26
    abuse of, 15, 20
    Brundtland Commission defini-
        tion, 2, 19, 24–25
    dynamism of, 16
    for Ehrenfeld, ix–x, 3–4, 6–7
    as emergent from workings of
        system, 18–19
    as flourishing, 6–7, 17–20, 22–24,
        36
    happiness as measure of, 21–22
    influences on Ehrenfeld's defini-
        tion of, 25–26
    as paradigm shift, 4–7, 15–16,
        20–21, 25, 54, 63, 127–28
    as possibility, 17–18, 22–23
    sustainable development and sus-
        tainable in relation to, 23
ConocoPhillips, 60
consumerism, 67–77
    corporate sustainability and, 42,
        54, 56, 67–68
    developing countries and, 68, 70,
        71–72
    economic behavior, need for
        change in, 120–22, 131–32
    human nature and, 73–75, 76
    inequality and, 72–73, 75

measuring human well-being
    and, 75–76
modern culture and, 76–77
moving away from, 69–70, 73–75
population growth and, 70–71
unsustainability of, 68–69
cormorants, 92
corporate social responsibility (CSR),
    50, 114
corporate sustainability, 2–3, 49–64
    as business strategy, 2–3, 53–54,
        62–63
    consumerism and, 42, 54, 56,
        67–68
    eco-efficiency as central organiz-
        ing principle of, 50–51
    economics and, 54–57
    future of, 122–25, 131
    human resources and, 96–97
    limitations of, 2–3, 49–51, 57–60
    reducing unsustainability versus
        creating sustainability, 54,
        58–59, 63
    sustainability scores or ratings,
        51–53, 60–62
    systems, Pragmatism and expe-
        riential learning in thinking
        about, 113–15
CSAs (community-supported agri-
    culture), 129
Csikszentmihalyi, Mihaly, 18
CSR (corporate social responsibil-
    ity), 50, 114
culture and sustainability. *See* mod-
    ern culture and sustainability

The Death of Nature (Merchant,
    1980), 105
defining sustainability. *See* concept of
    sustainability
Descartes, René and Cartesianism, 7,
    35–36, 46, 89, 101–2, 105, 119, 125

developing countries and consumerism, 68, 70, 71–72
Diamond, Jared, 85
The Dismal Science (Marglin, 2008), 41
dominance, 35–37, 45, 46
Douglas, Mary, 69
Drucker, Peter, 54, 59
DTE Energy, 60
Durkheim, Emile, 100

Earth Day, 60
The Ecology of Commerce (Hawken, 1993), 110
"Economic Man" *(Homo economicus)*, 5–6, 29–30
Economic Policy Institute, 55
economics. *See also* consumerism; corporate sustainability
    consumer behavior, need for change in, 120–22, 131–32
    corporate sustainability and, 54–57
    GDP, 30, 42, 50, 68, 70, 72, 75
    in modern culture, 29–31, 34–35, 39–43
education. *See* business education, *and specific schools*
Eearth (McKibben, 2010), 38
Ehrenfeld, John R.
    contributions to sustainability, vii–x, 1–10
    emotional responses to sustainability conundrum, 63–64, 126–27
    religious practices and beliefs, 45
energy renaissance, 128–29
Enlightenment, 4, 7, 21, 36, 46, 100, 105, 109
Enron, 4
"environmentally friendly," as term, 58

experiential learning, 102–4, 108–15
ExxonMobil, 60

"Fallacy of Misplaced Concreteness," 52
Farrell, Paul, 34
Fiji water, 60
fishing, 8, 92
flourishing, sustainability as, 6–7, 17–20, 22–24, 36
"flow," concept of, 18
football, head trauma in, 110
free market. *See* economics
Friedman, Milton, 131
Fromm, Erich, 7, 25, 83, 89
Fukushima Daiichi nuclear disaster, Japan (2011), 86
the future, 119–36
    business education and, 123, 128, 132–33
    components of new model for, 119–20
    consciousness, signs of change in, 127–31
    continuing feasibility of sustainability, 127–28
    corporate sustainability, evolution of, 122–25, 131
    economic behavior of consumers, change in, 120–22, 131–32
    optimism versus hope for, 39, 47, 55, 119, 125–27
    religion and spirituality, role of, 132–33
    young people as, 134–35

Gandhi, Mahatma, 5, 74
gardening, 9, 112
Gates, Bill, 72, 94
gay marriage, 130
GDP (gross domestic product), 30, 42, 50, 68, 70, 72, 75

Giddens, Anthony, 77
Gilding, Paul, 122
Glad Products Company, 60
global warming/climate change, 38, 60, 71, 110
GoodGuide, 52, 61–62
Great Depression, 30
Great Recession/global financial crisis of 2008, 4–5, 68–69, 99
green-washing, 57–58, 60
Greenbiz.com, 123
gross domestic product (GDP), 30, 42, 50, 68, 70, 72, 75
Gross National Happiness, 76
Gulf of Mexico, BP oil spill in, 4

happiness, 21–22, 41, 76
Harvard Business School, 120
Havel, Vaclav, 119, 126
Having versus Being, 7, 18, 25–26, 74, 83–84, 88, 89, 91–93, 99, 104, 106
Hawken, Paul, 110, 125
Heidegger, Martin, vii–x, 5, 25–26, 89, 95
Heilbroner, Robert, 54–55
Heinberg, Richard, 47, 68
Heraclitus, 40
Hollender, Jeffrey, 58
Homo economicus ("Economic Man"), 5–6, 29–30
hope versus optimism, 39, 47, 55, 119, 125–27
human nature, 81–97
    authenticity, 82–83, 86–87, 92–93, 95
    caring, 17, 25, 67, 74, 83–88, 89, 91–92, 105–6, 128, 131, 136
    Cartesian thinking and, 35–37, 46, 89
    consumerism and, 73–75, 76
    corporate sustainability and, 96–97

Having versus Being, 7, 18, 25–26, 74, 83–84, 88, 89, 91–93, 99, 104, 106
    leadership, 58, 74, 87, 93–95, 103, 134
    love, 8, 88–89, 90–91
    a new approach to sustainability issues, 81–82, 89–90
    "normal sustainable consumption," 82
    personal development programs, 95–96
    social interconnectedness, 85–89
    spirituality, 88
human well-being, measuring, 75–76

India, 4, 68, 71, 74
individuals. *See* human nature
inequality, 2, 9, 43, 50, 72–73, 75, 134
information technology, 33–34
interconnectedness
    social, 85–89
    in systems, 104–7, 125
Interface, Inc., 124–25
iPads, 74, 99
Iraq War, 51, 63
Jackson, Tim, 69

James, William, 7, 108–9
Japan, 86
Jobs, Steve, 94

Kant, Immanuel, 50
Kasser, Tim, 59, 69
Kennedy, John F., 37–38
Keynes, John Maynard, 54
Kotler, Philip, 59
Kuhn, Thomas, 4

Laing, R. D., 35
Land, Edwin, 95
Lasch, Christopher, 126

leadership, 58, 74, 87, 93–95, 103, 134
Leopold, Aldo, 5, 6
Lewin, Kurt, 95
Lifestyle of Health and Sustainability
    (LOHAS), 129
Limits to Growth (Meadows et al.,
    1972), 127
The Little Prince (Saint-Exupéry),
    135–36
LOHAS (Lifestyle of Health and
    Sustainability), 129
love, 8, 88–89, 90–91, 130
Lovins, Amory, 124

Makower, Joel, 1
Marglin, Steve, 41
market economics. *see* economics
Marlboro College Graduate Center,
    ix, 43, 90, 133
Maslow, Abraham, 5, 69, 84
Massachusetts Institute of
    Technology (MIT), viii, ix, 53, 71,
    120, 133
Maturana, Humberto, 5, 8, 36, 37,
    88, 102, 112
Max-Neef, Manfred, 31, 59
McDonough, Bill, 124
McKibben, Bill, 38
Meadows, Donella and Dennis, 90,
    127
mechanistic view of systems, 100–103
Merchant, Carolyn, 105
Merwin, William Stanley, 126
MIT (Massachusetts Institute of
    Technology), viii, ix, 53, 71, 120, 133
modern culture and sustainability,
    29–47
    Cartesian thinking and, 35–37, 46
    consumerism, 76–77. *See also*
        consumerism
    economics, dominance of, 29–31,
        34–35, 39–43

myths and models of, 32–35,
    37–38
religion and, 30, 36, 44–46
skewed values in, 29–32
technology in, 32–34, 38–39
work/life balance, 43–44

Native Americans, 106
neoclassical economics. *see*
    economics
Newsweek 500 greenest companies,
    51–52
Nigeria and Royal Dutch Shell, 4
Nike, 4
9/11, 51
"normal sustainable consumption,"
    82

Occupy movement, 5, 55, 69, 121, 130
"On the Realization of Human
    Potential: Path with a Heart"
    (Shepard, 1984), 92
optimism versus hope, 39, 47, 55, 119,
    125–27
The Organization Man (Whyte,
    1956), 5
Orr, David, 126
Our Common Future (Brundtland
    Commission Report), 2, 19
ozone layer, 39, 110

paradigm shift, sustainability as, 4–7,
    15–16, 20–21, 25, 54, 63, 127–28
Patagonia (outdoor clothing com-
    pany), 122–24
personal development programs,
    95–96
Pickett, Kate, 43
population growth, 70–71
Porter, Michael, 59
positive psychology, 89
possibility, 17–18, 22–23, 86

poverty and poverties, 31–32, 70
Pragmatism, 7, 103, 108–15, 136
Presidio Graduate School, San
    Francisco, 133
Prosperity Without Growth (Jackson,
    2011), 69
Putnam, Robert, 85

quantum mechanics, 133

Randers, Jorgen, 90
ratings or scores of sustainability,
    51–53, 60–62
reductionism, 33, 35, 46, 100, 101, 120
religion and spirituality, 30, 36,
    44–46, 88, 104–7, 132–33
Rio+20 conference, 128
Royal Dutch Shell, 4
Rumsfeld, Donald, 108

Saint-Exupéry, Antoine de, 135–36
A Sand County Almanac (Leopold,
    1949), 6
Sandel, Michael, 55
Sarkozy, Nicolas, 75
Scharmer, Otto, 93
schools of business. *See* business edu-
    cation, *and specific schools*
Schor, Julie, 69
Schumacher, E. F., 56, 59
scientific method, 38, 46, 100–102,
    104, 106, 108, 110–11
scores or ratings of sustainability,
    51–53, 60–62
Sen, Amartya, 32, 75
September 11, 2001, 51
Seventh Generation (company), 58
Shepard, Herbert, 92
Silent Spring (Carson, 1962), 106
Simon, Herbert, 40
Small is Beautiful (Schumacher,
    1973), 56

Smith, Adam, 41, 54, 121–22
social interconnectedness, 85–89
social media, 33–34, 128, 132
solidarity, 130
Soros, George, 55
The Spirit Level (Wilkinson and
    Pickett, 2010), 43
spirituality and religion, 30, 36,
    44–46, 88, 104–7, 132–33
Stieglitz, Joseph, 75
sustainability, 1–11
    as academic discipline, viii–ix, 1
    consumerism and, 67–77. *See also*
        consumerism
    corporate, 2–3, 49–64. *See also*
        corporate sustainability
    defining, 15–26. *See also* concept
        of sustainability
    Ehrenfeld's contributions to,
        vii–x, 1–10
    as flourishing, 6–7, 17–20, 22–24,
        36
    in the future, 119–36. *See also*
        future
    in individuals, 81–97. *See also*
        human nature
    mainstreaming of, 1–3
    modern culture and, 29–47.
        See also modern culture and
        sustainability
    as paradigm shift, 4–7, 15–16,
        20–21, 25, 54, 63, 127–28
    personal experience and, 7–9
    political stances on, 9–10
    as possibility, 17–18, 22–23, 86
    in systems, 99–115. *See also*
        systems
Sustainability by Design (Ehrenfeld,
    2008), ix
sustainable, as term, 23
sustainable development, as term,
    23, 127

systems, 99–115
   complexity of, 99–100, 102,
      107–8, 112, 119, 125
   corporate sustainability and, 113–15
   mechanistic view of, 100–103,
      105–6
   Pragmatism and experiential
      learning, 102–4, 108–15
   pre-Enlightenment view of, 105
   spirituality and interconnected-
      ness with, 104–7, 125

Tea Party, 5, 55, 69
technology in modern culture,
   32–34, 38–39
Theory U (Scharmer, 2009), 93
time banking, 130
To Have or To Be? (Fromm, 1976), 89
Toyota Production System, 94, 114
Triandis, Harry, 69
truth, 37–38, 112

UL Environment, 62
UN Millennium Ecosystem
   Assessment, 1–2

Underwriters Laboratory, 62
Union of Concerned Scientists, 60
United Kingdom, 130
United Nations, 2, 71, 72
University of Michigan, 120
U.S. Census data, 2

Walmart, 4, 50, 51, 54, 59–60, 132
Weber, Max, 104
Weick, Karl, 112
Welch, Jack, 59
Wellinghoff, John, 129–30
What Money Can't Buy (Sandel,
   2012), 55
White, Lynn, 45
Whitehead, A. N., 52
Whyte, William, 5
Wilkinson, Richard, 43
work/life balance, 43–44
World Business Council for
   Sustainable Development, 50
Worldcom, 4

Zuckerberg, Mark, 94